Dedicated to his posterity

& in memory of

Verl Irvin Page (1922-2015)

Compiled 2017 by Helena M. & Terri N. Page

On December 3, 1922, I, Verl Irvin Page, was born to James Irvin Page and Lareta McCombs in my Grandparents McCombs home at Riverdale, Idaho. This is about 10 miles from Dayton. I am the second child and first son.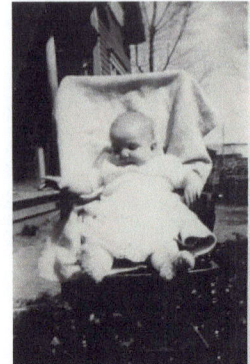
Verl in His Mother's Arms

My father rode a horse from Dayton to Riverdale that [Sunday] morning at 5:00am. [He had to ford the Bear River, East of Dayton on his horse to cross the valley through farmland which took an hour.][1] I was blessed Jan. 7, 1923 by John Waite. I lived in Dayton all my life. And I guess I growed up there, as much as I'll ever grow up. My dad ahead of me lived all his life in Dayton.

My second name, Irvin, is after my dad. Now, where they got the Verl from, I don't know. One thing I did learn, there weren't many Verls around there where I was growing up. I am the oldest living of five children. They are: Erland Don, Thelma and Keith M. The oldest child, Mary died at birth.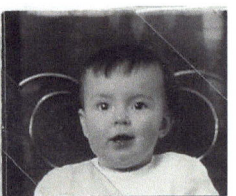

As a baby I and my family lived in the James Page home in Dayton. This home was located about a mile and a half north of the Dayton chapel. However, when I was just 2 years old we moved into a little log house that had two rooms in it. This is where Erland Don was born. We lived there then moved from

McCombs Home in Riverdale, Idaho

James Page Home

that house into other houses when I was a child we lived in, but I don't remember them.

We moved into what we called the Mickelsen place. It had been used for a post office. It had two doors on the front and they were big rooms. That's where my sister was born, in that home.

---

[1] Helena M. Page

I remember it, because it was big enough that we had room to play. We had a dog, called her Chip. She was a good cattle dog. I remember, when I wasn't very big, we play out on the front lawn and there was an irrigating ditch a crossed the front of there and we'd go out and play on the lawn. Don was just able to walk and that's about all. He kept trying to get in the ditch and that dog would stay between him and the ditch. I don't know how she knew what she was supposed to do, but  she'd stay between him and the ditch and he'd try to get around her.

Dad went up to the canyon to get our winter's wood one day and right after we left, the cows got out. My mother went out and the dog helped her get the cows back in the corral. Then the dog laid there where that fence was knocked down; laid there all day and when Dad got back that night the cows were still in the corral.

We sure loved that dog. It was funny how our lives were kinda based around that dog at that time.

While were living at the Mickelsen Home we wandered over to the store and got some candy. One day I went over to the store to get an all-day sucker. I got myself one and got a green one for my little sister, Thelma. When I got home, Mother sent me back to get a red one for Thelma. Mother was thinking if green apples got you sick, then green all day suckers would too!

Mickelsen Home

After Thelma was born then we moved back into the log house. I can remember taking these pictures of us on the porch of the log house. We had a post office about a half a block away from there. Don and I would go up and get the mail but my mother would always give us a flour sack or a sugar sack to carry the mail in. We'd go up and the post mistress would put the mail in that sack and then we'd carry it back home. That isn't that far, but it seemed like a long ways.

[That log house sat back off the main highway in Dayton. Across from where the City Building or park sits now. That same park is where we have our reunion.][2]

There were several other houses I remember, but in the spring of 1928 the family moved to the farm from the Waite Home.

---

[2] Helena M. Page

An early memory is when my father took me, at age 3, to the barn and taught me to hand-milk a pet Jersey cow. My grandparents gave my mother a cow when my dad and mother got married. A little Jersey cow. When she was about ready to dry up my dad said, "Ok, you can milk her." I milked her for a little while and she dried up.

On my sixth birthday, Dad got me up and started me to milk cows both morning and night milkings. Before this, I milked cows evenings only.

I was old enough to milk cows twice a day. From then on I milked cows night and mornings. This was done by hand. Oh, I'd better not tell you about it. I was little enough that they could kick me and hurt me. That's about the only thing I ever knew, was to milk cows.

I always had to feed calves. We had chickens, we had pigs that we had to feed, sheep, lambs. My job for a lot of years was taking care of the sheep when they were lambin'. That was part of my job. To get those lambs in under a heat lamp or into the house by the stove to warm them up. That was all right in the daytime, but in the nighttime I didn't really enjoy that. Boy, I had a lot of other chores I had to do. Dad always had horses, and they had to be fed and watered. Back at this time, we had a well down by the house and the barn was back there and the fields not very far from the well. But we had to get those horses in the wintertime and the well would go just about dry. What would happen, Dad would go out and draw that well dry just as quick as he would get up along about 4 or 5 o'clock in the morning. It was our job to get the horses up there and water them. And when they got a drink then we'd tie them back in the barn. Then we'd bring the young stock and draw the water up, put it in their trough and put them back in the corral. When we were done milking we'd go get the cows and bring them down to water. This was an all day job, just with the water being that low. Just had to keep drawing water when we could get it. I remember when we got the city water out there, and seemed good to go out there and turn the hydrant on and have the water running in there for 'em rather than having to pack it to 'em.

In the summertime, it was always... after I got big enough to help, six years and older, I used to have to follow my dad and help him irrigate. Back when we would water down the row on the beets. My job, most of the time, was to be on the bottom end of the field. When the water came through, my dad would turn it off and put the water in the next row. I would usually have to walk up through the field to tell him that it was done. 'Cause you couldn't shout loud enough to make him hear that far away. Now they use radios and cell phones to do all that kind of stuff, so we don't have any real problems any more.

One of the earliest things I can remember is when I was six years old. I started school and then quit it. Because I was young, well I was five turning six in December. I quit school and was home. And along in January we had a break, we kept the horses in one end of the barn, cows in the other end. A horse that Dad had bought was a big gray horse. We used to have chickens out in the barn and they'd lay the eggs along in the grain boxes. It's where the horses would get their grain. I climbed up to gather the eggs, and looking over the edge of the manger, this horse saw me coming up. And he just reached out and bit, my right cheek. The top piece hitting up at the corner of my eye, and the bottom going clear down to my lower jaw. I still have part of that scar. There were several of the neighbors out by the barn door talking to my father when they heard me yell and scream. They ran around the corner of the barn and saw me standing there with a chunk of my cheek in my hand. As I come out of the barn I remember having my hands, both hands, on that chunk, holding it. They took me partway to town in an iron-wheeled wagon. The Kirkbride car wouldn't start so they pulled it to the railroad depot. When they got down to the railroad station the agent, Mr. Bob Goodwin, saw us coming and he come over in his car. For several minutes, it seemed that I went around the depot several times. They loaded me in the car, and took me over to the doctor. The doctor laid this cheek up and there was 13 blood vessels cut off and three at the top of it hanging. All that was holdin' the skin on the top. My parents were scared that my cheek wouldn't live.

It took 13 stitches to sew that side of my cheek back in place. After surgery, I lived with my grandma, Mary Ann McCombs, in Preston. She lived about a block and a half from the doctor's office.

I walked to Dr. Cutler and Worley offices to have the wound cleaned and dressed. (Those offices were in a building where the Wells Fargo Bank now stands.) He kept worrying about these blood cells that'd been cut off. That's what they called them then. I think they're different now.

But any way, my aunt kept teasing me about my cheek dying. This whole chunk out of my cheek. This is back when you first started hearing about rubber tires and stuff. After that, my uncle was always kidding me about grafting in a rubber cheek. They says, "Oh, we'll have the doctor make you up a rubber cheek." They had a lot of fun with me. I took it serious.

Anyway later, before I got away from Grandma McCombs' place, my youngest uncle, Pete, bought me a box of colored chalk and a slate, or a chalkboard. When I played with the chalk, I got an infection in my face, taking longer for the wound to heal. It took longer to get this infection cleared up than it did to start with. Anyway, that went on for quite a while. I had to walk that block and a half every day up to the office over the bank building.

And we used to have to walk up the stairs. I always had someone walking right behind me to make sure I didn't tip over backwards.

Before I started school, at six years old, I had my tonsils removed as I could barely hear. I survived all the common childhood diseases during my growing up years. The diseases I have had are: chicken pox, scarlet fever, whooping cough and German measles. I have been inoculated for diphtheria and vaccinated for small pox.

One other thing that I remember is: We had a flood come down through there. We lived right next to a creek and it flooded out over the yard. Dad and Mother had a little banty hen out there, well, then it seemed like 30 little chicks. Those things were swimming around out in the water, they lost most of them. They saved a few of them, but most of them went with the flood. That's, as a kid, what I remember. There's a lot of others, but you ain't got time for all that.[3]

I had nick-name but never told anybody about it. I had a cousin come, and he remembered it but honored my wishes and never did tell the kids anything about it. I just never used it. I didn't like it, so I never used it. Or never let anybody know about it. That's for the nick-name. I always went by my first name. Other than that when I grew up, I had one neighbor that always called me my dad's name, Irvin.

In Don's recorded history, he tells that, "When I was about three, Verl and I were playing horses. He had a rope around my neck and tied me to the bar on the front of the coal stove in the kitchen. I pulled back and finally just hung myself. Mother saw me and got the barber scissors and cut the string. She said, 'The blood looked like it was ready to break the skin on my face when I finally fell to the floor.' She was surprised I was still alive."

"When I was four years old, we had a cow that was very gentle and I used to milk on one side and Verl the other. On my seventh birthday, Dad said that made me old enough to milk regular so every morning from then on at 6:00 am Dad woke me to do chores. Again at night, I helped milk. We usually milked between eight and 14 cows. At about that time I started thinning beets and Mother used to space with a long handled hoe and I crawled behind pulling weeds and double beets."[4]

---

[3] Elizabeth Page, Young Women's Interview, Dec. 30, 2003
[4] Don & Hazel Page Personal Histories, 1996

Sometime in my early life, I went over to my Grandparents McCombs home for Thanksgiving Dinner. They had turkey and it was really a treat. It seemed as though I would never get that turkey drumstick finished. It seemed like it was a foot long.

Before we moved to the farm, Dad would drive the cattle down to the farm while he worked all day and then bring them back and milk them at night. After we got down on the farm, we got busy building corrals. The house we lived in only had two little bedrooms and a front room and a kitchen were just partitioned off a little bit. They weren't two complete rooms. If you went in the kitchen you had to back out. You couldn't turn around in there, it was that small.

The thing I remember the most about that was the bed bugs. Those tiny bed bugs, Dad would fumigate that house, we'd go live off in what we used for a garage out behind, and we'd stay there all day and a night. Go in and clean the house out again, it seemed like it happened every year. We'd have bed bugs, they'd move back in. It got to where it was almost too embarrassed to go to church, because one of those dang bed bugs might be crawling on the back of your neck or something. It was just something that everybody, most people had. So even though it was embarrassing, it was something that could happen to anybody. I remember one night instead of staying home, this was after we got the Model A Ford. We decided that we was going to do the chores and we'd go down to Clarkston and stay with his sister down there. We stayed there that night. Next morning we was up and got packed just before it got daylight. We was coming home and there was a fellow in a suit out by a haystack; he'd been partying all night. Just as a kid that sure impressed me.

More on that, it was just about the same time, Dad wanted us to see what the other kind of life was like. They had a pool hall over there in Preston and he picked a good time. He took us over there one Saturday night and guys were partying, boozing and this one guy was in there throwing up. Anyway when he got us home he sat us down at the table there and we visited a bit and he said, now do you want to live like that? You can, or you can live like, he pointed out our bishop and a few other upstanding neighbors. Or you can live like this. It's just going to be up to you how to decide I'm not going to tell you how you gotta live. That night at the pool hall was enough to tell us what we wanted to do. He just took me and my brother, my youngest brother the baby then. That's been a lesson that really stuck. I don't know why he took us to the pool hall, I don't remember him ever going to the pool hall. He may have done, but I don't remember it.

One thing I remember about the pool hall, was after topping beets with a neighbor. This one neighbor always had to go to town take his eggs to town every Saturday and then he'd go to the pool hall and play pool all afternoon. His wife would walk the streets, she'd come walking along the streets and if she'd see me she'd want me to go in and get him. Well, that was alright, for a while, but pretty soon I got to feeling, hey, I don't want to be seen in there. So when I'd see her coming I'd duck off into a store or something so she didn't see me. But it was a good lesson, might have been a hard way to teach it but, it's something that has always stuck with me.

Now, what I first remember, we used to travel in a team and wagon. Now this is a lumber wagon. My dad didn't have a buggy. Then, later when winter would come, we would hitch on to a bobsled usually. I don't really remember my dad ever having a wagon box. We always had what's called a dump board. That's just several boards across the bottom and two wide boards sitting up the side and end gates. And that was our way of traveling in the winter times. And that was alright, until they got started using cars. Cars got the roads so slick, the horses had a hard time standing up to pull the sleigh.

That's the way we traveled until my dad bought a Model T Ford. When we traveled in the Model T, the first I can remember, my mother would hold my sister on her lap, and younger brother would sit up on a kind of a shelf behind Mother. And I'd sit up on that shelf behind Dad and we'd have our feet together.

Don remembers that they sat that way until they "were big enough they had to bend way over all the time they were riding. After that we drove a team and wagon or sleigh everywhere we went except Verl and I rode a saddle horse to church each Sunday. That was about a mile and a half from home. There were a couple of boys that used to chase us. They were two or three years older than Verl and they would ride up and pull us off from the horse and many times  ruined our clothes. So one day Dad said, 'Take this whip and use it on the horse and whip on the horse and out run them.' The never bothered us again."[5]

I don't remember a lot of traveling in a car. I don't remember if he bought a used one or whether we bought it new. But that was the way we got around.

---

[5] Don & Hazel Page Personal Histories, 1996

After the car quit us we went back to horse and wagon, unless we were going to church. And we'd ride up there in the sleigh or wagon and take it to what they called a hitchin' post out in front and tie the horses up and go to church. That's about all I remember about that one.

School Daze

I started grade school in 1928. My teachers were: First Grade – Ann Hansen; Second and Third Grade – Miss Nelson; Fourth and Fifth Grades – Leonard Roskelly; Sixth and Eighth Grades – Howard Nelson; Seventh Grade – LeRoy Archibald. I went to Weston for my four years of High School. My favorite High School class was shop, where I learned woodworking.

I was baptized at Sunset Springs, in Dayton on 25 April 1931.

My dad, James Irvin Page baptized me. He was assigned to do the baptisms for the whole ward. And this time there was one other fellow and a cousin of mine that he baptized and this was the first part of April. He hadn't opened the swimming pool down next to the river, the hot water well down there, there were several of them, but they let us go into the swimming pool and they filled it so we didn't get baptized in ice water, it was fairly warm. Others who were there, I think that just my dad and these other two boys the same age as I was. It was different, but I'm sure glad we didn't have to go out and break a hole in the ice! I was confirmed 3 May 1931 by Albert Walker.

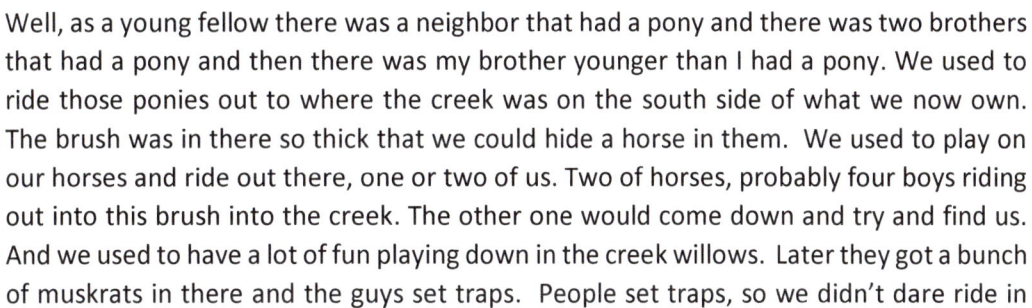

I shook hands with President Heber J. Grant at the dedication of the Dayton Ward Chapel on 15 Nov 1930.

Well, as a young fellow there was a neighbor that had a pony and there was two brothers that had a pony and then there was my brother younger than I had a pony. We used to ride those ponies out to where the creek was on the south side of what we now own. The brush was in there so thick that we could hide a horse in them. We used to play on our horses and ride out there, one or two of us. Two of horses, probably four boys riding out into this brush into the creek. The other one would come down and try and find us. And we used to have a lot of fun playing down in the creek willows. Later they got a bunch of muskrats in there and the guys set traps. People set traps, so we didn't dare ride in there while they were out trapping muskrats. That was the fun we had.

Dayton Ward Chapel. MARCH 1956

We had to use the horses to herd the cows, but we had to have time for fun too. Herding cows wasn't really all that bad cause we had our ponies to ride. We would usually round up all the neighbors' cows and our own cows, so we quite enjoyed it. Of course the neighbors would pay us a little money for herding.

[When Verl was about 10 or 11 years old, he wore his father's shoes to the canyon to get their winters wood because his shoes were worn out. Irvin wore his irrigating boots.][6]

Did I ever have any embarrassing moments? Stupid things, but I don't know if I was embarrassed or not. I think the thing that bothered me the most was when I would do something and Dad would question me about it. I guess it was alright, but he disciplined pretty heavy and I learned then that if I didn't want him to know about it, I just kept my mouth shut.

I graduated Primary and was ordained a deacon on 9 Dec. 1934. I became a boy scout on 29 Dec. 1934.

I never, never enjoyed school, probably why is 'cause we usually had the fall harvest, with beets, and we'd work until school had been going for about six weeks and then I'd try to get into school and find out that I didn't know what the rest of the kids were talking about. But, really I didn't like to study and that's probably why, I didn't like school.

Really the only classes that I enjoyed was when I was in eighth grade, we had a teacher by the name of Howard Nelson that taught us spelling, well the other subjects too, but I don't remember them 'cause I didn't learn them I guess. In spelling he'd give us a folded sheet of paper, folded in four like an accordion. The first one was the words, on the front of it. All spelled out so we could read them. Then he'd ask for the definition on the second page and on the third page, he'd explain a little more about why they were spelled how they were spelled and then on the back page you just wrote them on. All you had to do was remember. I won't say I enjoyed it, but I did learn how to spell. I never learned anything to spell after that.

---

[6] Helena M. Page, 2016

Talking about teachers that I liked it was mostly the ones after I got in High School in the shop. Wood working shop, I had two teachers that taught me how to do wood work. And one of them was just a little bit of a guy, I was in High School but I think it was in my junior year, I was a head taller than he was. He just had a way of appealing to me. I could do about anything he asked in shop. I could do it and I answered his questions. But that's probably why I didn't like school was they'd ask me questions, and I didn't know what they were talking about. I did learn arithmetic; I got along pretty good with that. I had one heck of a time with algebra, how I got through that was just because I knew the shop teacher and he was teaching it. The thing with him, if I didn't understand a problem, we'd get about four or five of us and each one of us would take turns going up and having him work out a problem. That way we get them all.

"Later in years, Grandpa would out figure me even though I did well in school. He could take and see a stack of hay and figure out how many tons of hay was in the stack. He could figure out how to do that, I couldn't do that. He could figure out how many acres in a field, and he knew how to figure in his head a lot faster than I could. I think I can do it as fast as he can now, but originally he could do it better than I could. So even though he said he didn't do well in school, he still could do things that he doesn't give himself credit."[7]

I did take band when I was young. And I don't know that I really enjoyed that. Dad kinda insisted that the kids get some music in their lives. So I did take band, and I did play baritone. And then later, I think it was my senior year I gave up band. I didn't go on any kinds of trips that they take now days. I liked the wood working part. I got along fine in that part. Didn't do too much school activity, because when they played basketball I had eczema really bad on my legs. When I'd put shorts on to play basketball the kids would tease me about having to itch. So it didn't

Dayton Ward Recreation Hall

---

[7] Helena M. Page

take long for me to find out I didn't particularly need to play basketball. Not that I didn't like to, I just didn't do it. And to kinda fill in, they got a roller skating rink. And we used to like to go there and skate. I spent a lot of time skating; every Thursday night we would go up there and skate. And that's where I was still skating there when I met your mother, grandmother. But ah.... I enjoyed that skating, I don't know whether she did or not. I could always keep us both up.

In May 1941, I graduated from High School.

At about the time I graduated, I was put in as an assistant YMMIA secretary and assistant scout master.

Mother

At the time, Keith was born, Mother became sick and was sick most of the time for the next 10 years. The last 10 years of her life, my mother always stayed in her bedroom. When we came into the house, we would wash up and go in to talk to her.

Thelma related the following, "Mother was sick in bed the day we moved the old house off the foundation to start to build the new house, September 1937. We moved into the new house January 13, 1938. Mother died on December 20, 1938, at the age of 39."

"Before Dad built the new house, he would draw floor plans on any piece of paper he could find, every time he came in for dinner. Roy Walker was from Clifton. He built houses for a living. Dad asked him to build the new house. Roy told Dad he was too busy with the work he already had promised. But his son Zane wanted to learn more. Roy would tell Zane what to do each day. So Dad, Verl, Don and Zane built the new house."[8]

Don said, "The old house was so small that Verl and I slept in a tent all that summer and fall and in December during a blizzard our tent tore in half and by morning we were covered with snow. That day we moved into the basement of the new house although there were not windows or doors on the house. We worked hard and long hours to get it closed in. When it was almost finished, Dad ran out of money and needed $100.00 to get it finished so we could move in. He sold our four best cows to get the $100.00."

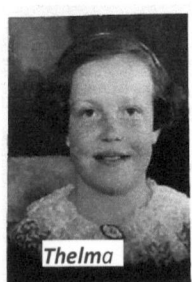

Thelma continues, "When we kids were in school, if Dad was going to be working around the yard, then we went to school. Otherwise, one of us stayed home to be with Mother. She was bedridden. I stayed home more than 30 days when in the sixth grade. The School Board made a rule if a child missed 30 days or more they could not pass on to the next grade. My teacher said it was not my fault I missed so many days, so he passed me anyway. My brothers would get my lesson assignments from the teacher and I would do them. Then my brothers would take them to the teacher."

---

[8] Thelma Page Stone

"Mother had kidney and heart problems. When the doctor gave her medicine for her heart, it made her kidneys worse and when the dr. gave her medicine for her kidneys, it made her heart worse. They called it 'Dropsy' back then. Now it is heart failure."

"I learned to cook, do laundry, iron, mend clothes, can fruits and vegetables. I learned to do everything a wife did to take care of her home and family. I was 11 ½ and 12 ½ years old. After we moved into the new house, Mother was sick most of the time. She would plan the meals and I would cook them."

"We had a little radio for the family. Dad would turn it on every night at 9:00 pm. It would sing "Happy Days are Here Again." We went to bed at 9:00pm and got up at 5:30 in the morning, so we could get work done by 8:30 am and go to school."

"When I was 16, I was the only girl in the Stake to receive the Golden Gleaner Award. They had different categories to work on. One was make your bed every day for a week, Iron a shirt, darn a pair of socks and many other things I was doing it all every week."

"I made eight big loaves of bread every other day. We ate bread and milk and canned fruit most of the time for supper. Otherwise, it was oyster soup or tomato soup."

"Dad's sisters, Cora, Alexis, and Rhonda always came and helped can corn, string beans and peas, because they didn't trust me using the pressure cooker until I got older."

"Mother always embroidered her dishtowels, pillow cases and top sheet and her bed jacket. A bed jacket had long sleeves, was waist length and tied at the neck with a pretty ribbon bow. It was worn over her nightgown. So she would look nice if anyone came to see her. Everything that was embroidered was ironed. Mother also knew how to crochet."

"Mother sewed most of my dresses. She had a treadle sewing machine. After Mother died, Aunt Alexia used Mother's clothes to make dresses for me. My hair was red and I had fair skin that would burn, so Mother always put clothes with long sleeves and a hat on me every time I went outside."

"Dad would take us for Sunday drives. It gave Mother a chance to get out of the house."

"When I was 10, Mother, Dad and Grandma McCombs and I went to the April Conference in the tabernacle in Salt Lake. We stayed in the hotel or motel. After that I always loved to listen to Conference, even if it was on the radio."

"Mother would applique and embroider quilt blocks for a sun bonnet girl quilt. She quilted it. One of the trips to the hospital, they put her on a plank of wood and wrapped that quilt around her. The nurses really liked that quilt."

"Mom was very bashful. As a young woman, she was afraid to go to mutual because she was worried that they would ask her to pray. Her friend promised if they asked Lareta to pray, she would do it for her."

"In January (I think 1936), Mother wrote this prayer out when Dad went to California with Ray Archibald, Jack Archibald and Dan Godfrey. They were gone for one month. It was January, Mother wanted each of us to memorize it before Dad got home."

> 'Our Father in Heaven, we thank Thee for life, health and strength and ask Thee to bless us in the future as you have done in the past. Bless the General Authorities of the church that they may be able to do the work in a pleasing manner before thee. Bless the missionaries with health and strength and lead them to the doors of the honest in heart. Bless all those that are sick at this time. Also those that are weary and sad. Take us in Thy care, that no harm may befall us. Bless this food it may do us the good we need and thank Thee for it. In the name of Jesus Christ, Amen.'

"Mother and Dad always took a car load of people to the temple in Logan. Many times it was the widows of the ward. They always bought a pound of candy for the ride home. The people in the car would eat a couple of pieces. What was left over they gave to us kids. We each got one piece and then we put it away. The next day when we kids wanted candy we each took one piece and put the rest away. We could make that candy last a long time."

"Birthdays Mother would always bake us a cake and decorate it with our names on it. After Mother died, I don't remember getting a cake or celebrating birthdays."

"We could get into the movies for a dime. We got to see most or all of the Shirley Temple ones. We didn't get popcorn or candy. The movie was our treat."

"Keith was a baby that cried a lot. Dad would come in and hold him so Mother could fix dinner. The neighbors would come and help with Keith."

"When we kids were young, Dad tried to borrow money from the bank for us new shoes for the winter. The banker said no. Dad was really disappointed. Dad thought about it and decided he'd better get some insurance on us kids in case one of us died, he would have money to bury us. Dad took out a $500.00 policy on each of us for a nickel a day. The insurance guy would come once a month to pick up the money."

Grandma McCombs and Lareta Page

"We rode the sleigh with the horses in the winter. We warmed rocks all night in the oven, put them in the bottom of the sleigh and put burlap over the rocks and put heavy quilts over the top of us. That kept us warm. We would go over to Grandma McCombs, put the rocks in the oven, do shopping and visit with Grandma awhile, put the rocks back in the sleigh and ride home."

"Grandma McCombs always wanted the runt piglet from Dad. She would feed it. She had one cow, and she milked it. She kept enough milk for her and a few neighbors. She fed the rest to the pig. The pig grew fast. It grew a lot faster than Dad's pig did."

"Mother was a visiting teacher when she was well enough. Mother was always happy. She didn't have a temper. She was very kind and patient. When it was in the spring, the Church windows were open and we could hear everyone singing the opening hymn. Mother said I won't go in late, so we went home. She was about 5' 2", 130 lbs., and long, brown hair."

"About two years before mother died, she got very sick. Dad's sisters came and prayed for her. She was in a coma for maybe two days then she got better. When Grandma McCombs came to stay with her, Mother told Grandma she had gone to a beautiful place. She said she had talked to Dad's mother and father and her father. Mother said she looked for baby Mary (Mother and Dad's first child), but she didn't see any babies. (We understand they are all full grown spirits). Grandma cried, so Mother told her not to tell Irvin about what they had talked about, because it would only make him worry. After Mother died Grandma told Dad about it. He said he wished he could have talked to her about it. He had several questions he wanted to ask her."

Thelma and Keith

"Mother wanted to stay in that beautiful place, but they told her she could not stay. Irvin and her children needed her. Mother got well rather rapidly after that."

"The day Mother died, she asked Dad to leave one of the older boys with her. Don was chosen to stay. The rest of us went to school. Keith was 10 years old, I (Thelma) was 12 years old, Don was 14 years old and Verl was 16."[9]

Don tells us that, "Mother by this time was quite sick. After we moved in, we took Mother for a ride in the car and let her see the house from all sides and I think that is the only time she was ever outside after moving in to the new home. A couple of years

---

[9] Thelma Page Stone, Sept. 2016, 90 years old

before Mother died, Dad finally had to hire a lady to come and help care for her. Anytime the lady wanted to be off, we children would take turns staying home with Mother. Just a night or two before she died, she came to the front room to see the Christmas tree and to sit in the new rocking chair we had got her for Christmas."

"I remember well, I stayed with her on December 19th and the morning of the 20th. It was Thelma's turn to stay home that day but Mother said she wanted Don. Dad said Don shouldn't stay too often but finally agreed I could stay. After breakfast, I left her to rest and went on with my play in the kitchen. At noon I looked in and she seemed to be resting. In about an hour the mail came and I took it to her but she had passed away."

"We didn't have a telephone so I ran to the neighbors and they went a mile to the railroad depot and reached Dad in Preston. At the time Dad was working for the County Road Commission. I guess the shock of being with Mom when she died made me sick, because by the morning of the 24th, I was so sick they wanted to leave me home from the funeral, but I wanted to go so bad. They let me go. After the funeral, we went to Aunt Alexia Chapman's for Christmas and I went to bed and stayed all evening and all of Christmas day. I don't remember whether it was longer or not."[10]

"Her funeral and burial was December 24, 1938."

"It was Christmas time, so the Christmas tree was at the end of her casket. They brought her to the house the day before the funeral. Early the morning of the funeral day, Keith and I (Thelma) touched her. I was not afraid of a dead person after that. Keith and I went to Aunt Alexia home after the funeral. Dad, Don and Verl got our Christmas presents and

stayed there all night. Aunt Alexia found cotton socks for all the kids except me. She gave me a nylon stocking. Everyone got about the same amount of candy except me. I got twice as much because the nylon kept stretching."

"I got my last baby doll and guitar that Christmas."

"That was the last year we had a Christmas tree. After that we just put Christmas lights around the window."

"When we lived in the little house, we had a little tree that we put on the sewing machine. The tree was three or four feet tall. We had small purchased decorations."

"Christmas in the new house we had a tree from floor to ceiling. We put electric lights on it. We kids decorated the tree. We put red rope from all four corners of the ceiling and a red paper bell in the center. After Mother died we kids started decorating it the same way, Dad came in, looked at it and started to cry. We stopped decorating."

"After mother died, Dad hired a housekeeper, Edith Bowman. She had never married, but she had a child. She was there for about six months. We as a family decided she was

---

[10] Don & Hazel Page History 1996

too fussy. She didn't like Dad to come in the house with his work clothes on and sit. So Dad decided he could live in a little dirtier house. So, he let her go. It was my job to take care of the house after that. I washed the dishes and Keith dried them. Keith would take the towel and throw it over the door, pretending it was a basketball, going through a hoop."

"Whenever Dad was sick, he would call out for my mother. He carried a picture of Lareta in his suit coat all of his life."[11]

Childhood

Well, as a young kid, we used to play fox and geese out in the snow. That used to be our exercise I guess after we got the chores done at night. Probably the most fun that I can remember is when… well, this is later in life, probably 12 or 13 years old. They was just learning that they could make rubber wagon wheels out of old cars or trucks. I had an uncle [Hyrum] with a Willis-Knight truck. He had the seat taken out, had it all stripped down to just the steering wheel. We, along with our cousins, used to push that up on the side hill and ride it down. And right at the bottom, where it comes out of the road or out of the lane, there was a main highway, Yellowstone Highway went past there. When we'd push that up sometimes there'd be a car coming. There was a big ditch and a row of trees along there. If there was a car coming, we'd turn that thing over or the driver would turn it over and hit the ditch and the trees. Kids flying every direction. Why some of us didn't get killed, I don't know. But we had a lot of fun doing it.

These same cousins had a pony they called Piggy. We used to hook her and Shaz on a buggy they had and just ride her around through the orchard and stuff. Reach up in the trees and grab apples. Just fun things the kids could do. I think that that's about the size of the fun things. We all had chores that had to be done, and it seemed like that cut into our fun time. If there was any fun time, Dad usually found some more chores for us to do.

I'll tell you, I start telling about Christmas, that was our main fun day in the winter time. And we were real fortunate. I don't ever remember when there wasn't gifts for each one of the kids. In our home, there were only the four of us. We always got a gift. We had neighbors; I remember the one neighbor who a little girl and she had got for Christmas a little bag of unpopped popcorn. 'Course, I think she was just as happy with that as I was with my toy. We felt so bad for her.

Keith

To think that we had, we didn't have a lot of toys. But usually each one of the family would get a toy or Thelma would get a doll. The thing I remember about Christmas is later, when I was a teenager. Well I wasn't that old, about eight or nine. My brother and I each got a little red dump truck. It had a crank and handle on it that we could dump.

---

[11] Thelma Page Stone, Sept. 2016, 90 years old

We played all day. My younger brother got a little truck and the hoist on it was on a spring. When you tripped that, it dumped. It would go up itself. We had to crank ours up but his would go up. But he played with it all day and didn't know it would dump. That night he got in bed, and when he got in bed, he caught the handle that trips the spring on it. So the in bed clothes it dumped. He was screamin', "It's a dumpin', it's a dumpin', it's a dumpin'." We sure had a lot of fun with that. But it seemed like the candy always run out on Christmas day, candy and nuts. I remember after I was a teenager one morning we got up on New Year's Day and there's a sack of nuts sitting in the middle of the table. We thought Santa Claus had come back. Fact, that's what we'd decided among my brothers and sister. Santa had brought that. I guess he did, 'cause we sure enjoyed it.

We never celebrated birthdays after Mom died. We just grew older. We never knew anything about parties for birthdays when I was a kid. Probably some of them did, but not in our family.

Well, we didn't think of them as traditions. But the thing I remember probably the most, we always had family prayer by kneeling down around the table. I don't know what you would want to call it that or not. That was every morning. It seemed like on holidays, we'd after Dad got his car, his Model T, we used to take a ride around the area sometimes. The thing I remember the most was going over to Bear Lake. My sister had whooping cough, so we couldn't mix with people, you know for the holiday. So, we'd go for a ride in the car. Went over to Bear Lake and we'd wind up around the dug way to get over there. And she'd got sick and was throwing up and we couldn't stop, so Mother had her apron, she put it up around her face until we could get up around to where we could pull off the side of the road. We went over to Bear Lake and they were having a celebration over there we sat out and watched one of them, they had a little rodeo going. That seemed to be the tradition with us, we always had somebody sick or quarantined when there was a holiday; we'd mostly just get in the old car and go for a ride

Well, I never learned to read that good. And I imagine you can count all the books I've read on the fingers of one hand. I just read words or even sometimes just the letters in it. I never could read fast enough to hold the thoughts so I never got real enthused about reading. But I did like to be out in the area, out in the yards and the fields. I enjoyed that, even though it was hard work and that it was something I could do.

[After Verl had to quit working on the farm, he began to read the scriptures and the newspaper regularly. He kept his scriptures under his pillow.][12]

In 1943, I remember high school age my best friend, Lyman Jensen. His older brother was building a house. They moved the house in, they were going to pour a cement foundation and set the house on it. Then they decided to put a basement under it. He had a John Deere tractor. His brother did and they were inching that on a slip scraper to guide that dirt up from under the house. Lyman was driving the tractor. The John Deere tractor had a hand clutch on it. When his brother dragged the scraper back in, they'd load up the dirt and this friend of mine would pull it out with a tractor. This one time he backed in, and

---

[12] Helena M. Page

when he got back there he pushed the clutch forward to engage and he got back right against the house. He tried to stop that thing and he bumped the house with his back and that engaged that and it just jammed the steering wheel in his stomach. He was hurt seriously. And just tore him all up. They took him to the hospital He lived for about a week to 10 days and then he died. It was very sad, because he was my closest friend.

So I wound up with this one friend for a long while and I wasn't really that popular in school. Just because like I said before, about the eczema and kids kinda shied away from it. I don't blame 'em; that's just the way we was raised. But this other friend, his dad was a sheep herder. Just to make it short, easy to say, Bill Ward, he hadn't gone to school that much, so we got along real good. He was my friend. I didn't have any more friends. That's the way summer or winter, either one that was our friendship was, we did things together.

I remember my mother died when I was 16, and she had food that was stored away in what we called a fruit room. I remember she had some tapioca balls about the size of BB that you shoot in the BB guns. We had a bottle of them down there. He came out there one day. My dad and his brother in law, some of the kids went with them to get a load of straw. Bill and I was left to get dinner for the bunch. Bill liked to cook. I'd had all of the cooking I wanted while Mother was sick and then after she died. It seemed like the one that got hungry had to go in and cook dinner. So about the easiest way to do that was to go in and throw a dozen eggs in a pot and boil them. And that way we lived. But anyway, he seen that bottle of tapioca, down there. He said, "Can we use that?" I said, "Sure."

We took it up and he cooked it and we served that for dessert. And I still can't believe that he knew that much about that. I don't know where he learned it because there weren't many people that could afford that back then. But we enjoyed that meal. Enjoyed not having to haul the straw.

How did I discover talents as I grew up? I don't know that I ever discovered them. There's a few; I don't know how to answer that. Like I said, most of my thoughts, entertainment and everything else were centered around the farm. I learned a few

Clyde and Marva

things there that probably helped me get along. I got a loader, remember when we used to clean the corrals out, it was always done by hand. Loaded up on a spreader or wagon, first it with a wagon, then we finally got a spreader. In doing that we always seemed like we were busy enough. We didn't have time to go out get into mischief like some of my good friends. We was busy enough so that we didn't have time to think about all of the bad things that we could do. And I guess, it kinda stayed with me, only I got some bad habits lately now.

I think probably the best talent I had was learning to drive a tractor. I don't want to brag, but I got where I could handle that tractor pretty good. Even to the point that Dad had always scolded me 'cause I couldn't drive the horses and make them do what he wanted them to do. But I got even with him. After we got to the point on the farm we got the old four- wheel-drive truck, [He] used to get that thing stuck. So one year, we always decorated the old church house and used to go way up in the air and Dad took that old truck up to put a ladder in it, to put the wire and lights up. Anyway, this was back when I was still in school. I got home from school that night, and he said, "That truck is stuck there at the church house and I would like you to go up and get it out." I was happy to go. I was outside, of course [with] four-wheel-drive everybody thought there wasn't anything that could stop it. You get out in the snow and high centered the thing and they couldn't get it out. They wanted me to drive it out, all four wheels were caught in the air spinnin'. Anyway, I finally got a log chain, wrapped it around the front wheels 'cause they have power in them. We were out there for I guess an hour trying to get that out, but I did get it out. From then on, I never had any problem with Grandpa (Irvin) telling me how to drive the horses.

[Verl attended school in Dayton form 1929-1937. He graduated from Weston High School in 1941. He spent his years after high school working on his father's farm. Both his father and younger brother, Keith had hernia surgeries so Verl was exempt from military service in WWII, he was needed on the farm. His brother Don served.][13]

---

[13] Helena M. Page

Military Experience

I enlisted in the United States Maritime Service in Salt Lake City, on Jul. 19, 1945 and left for Basic Training as a Merchant Seaman at Catalina Island off the coast of Los Angeles, California, for about a month until Aug. 23, 1945. I sailed from Wilmington, California along the coast to San Francisco, Portland, Oregon and Seattle, Washington, as a water-tender on an oil tanker, S.S. Idaho. Then I sailed to Alaska and the Aleutian Islands, to Pearl Harbor and Honolulu on the Island of Oahu, and Hilo on the Island of Hawaii until Mar. 18, 1946. I sailed on the S.S. Arkansas as a wiper for a time then returned home to Dayton, Idaho that summer.

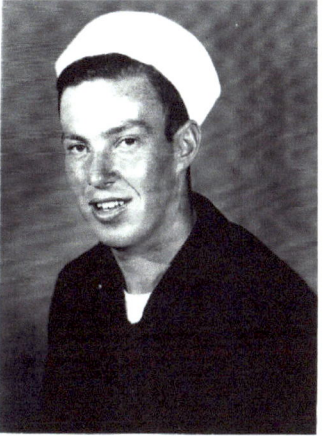

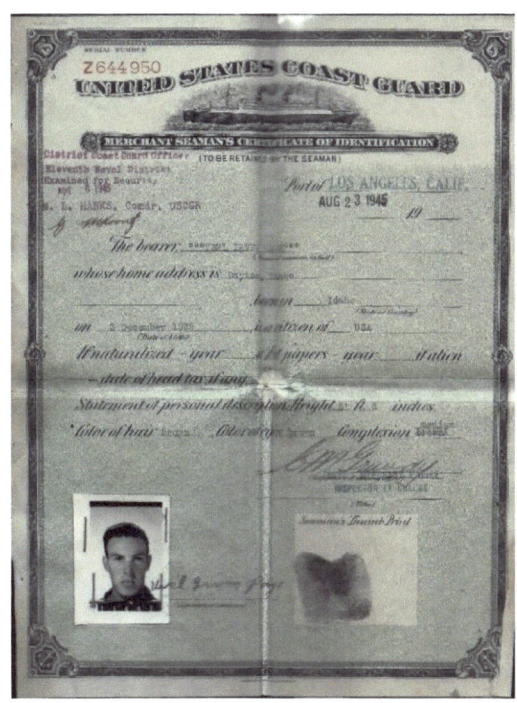

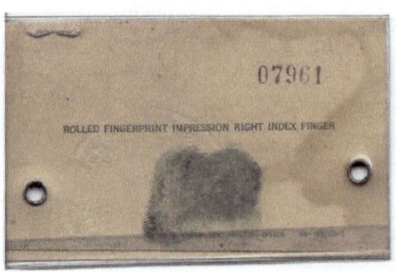

WAR EMERGENCY TANKERS, INC.
GENERAL AGENT
WAR SHIPPING ADMINISTRATION
80 BROAD STREET
NEW YORK 4, N. Y.
SS Idaho
March 18, 1946

To Whom it may concern:

This is to certify that Verl I. Page has served as Watertender on the above named ship from August 23rd., 1945 to March 18th., 1946.

During this time I have found him to be sober, and a willing worker.

He is leaving the ship of his own accord.

Respectfully,

H. E. McCracken
Ch. Engineer,
SS Idaho

United States Maritime Service
Release from Active Duty

This is to certify that PAGE, Verl Irwin 4907-11651 has been released from active duty on AUG 23 1946, at U.S. MARITIME SERVICE GRADUATE STATION, WILMINGTON, WILMINGTON, CALIFORNIA and placed in an inactive status in the United States Maritime Service.

Original enrollment at Salt Lake City, Utah on July 19, 1945

Regular enrollment at ____ on ____
Recalled for active duty at ____ on ____
Transportation furnished from ____ to ____ upon release from active duty.

Verl I. Page
(Signature of enrollee)

Official in Charge

Courtship

"We actually met at church. Everything in the community was centered around church. They had dances every Saturday night, which was kind of the typical thing during World War II time. I love to dance. I'm not a real good dancer but I always liked to."

"As a new school teacher in town, I just would come to the dance alone and then would dance with whomever you know would dance and I was welcomed into the community. They did that back in those days you don't hear much about that today."

"When you were the new school teacher in town everybody wanted to know who you were and knew more about you than you knew yourself, almost. Because it was such a small town."

"I came to Dayton to teach school to upper teens. Verl taught me how to skate. This was in the old recreation or amusement hall. It was behind the church house there in Dayton. We skated every week. That was our date, I guess. It wasn't really a date. I was there and he was there and he took me around the floor skating. And I'm not sure it was an actual date, but I don't remember for sure."[14]

The first one wasn't. But I thought they was. But anyway, one thing that happened there. I wasn't really good, but I did get so I could skate backwards. I had one friend that got him a pair of shoe skates, and wondered then why he could skate so much better than I could. He let me borrow them one night. Them shoe skates just glide with you the way you leaned on them and that. There wasn't nothing wrong with the shoes. They didn't glide around as good as them. One thing I guess I dare tell it. I was skating with another girl. She came there skating and I was skating with her and we were just having a pretty good time. And somebody came in and said that Helena Murri was over in Preston. She'd come in on the bus and she wants you to come and get her.

---

[14] Helena M. Page

This gal I was skating with didn't hear this, but anyhow I finally excused myself, and went and I got her and brought her over there. I didn't dare take her skating that night. I brought her home. Not my home, I don't think she ever knew that.

"We dated beginning about Nov 1944 through that school year, generally roller skating. He was an excellent skater. We would meet at the hall. We may have gone to a few movies in Preston, but not too sure about that."

"After school let out in the spring of 1945, I went back home to Newdale. Verl came up once bringing his cousin, Lucile Chapman, of Firth and his sister, Thelma to visit. This was just before Verl joined the Merchant Marines in Jul. Until he returned home in Mar. 1946, we corresponded with each other."

"I felt it was meant for us to be married when we first met. Valentines of 1946, I sent him this Valentine, while he was aboard his ship. He must have liked it because he kept it."[15]

Helena had two great uncles who lived in Dayton. After I'd started dating Helena, we had a project, a building project that was landscaping the grounds around the church house. These two uncles of hers were there I was running the loader.

My dad had a loader tractor we would load the dirt and then we'd haul a load around the church house. This great uncle, Lon Cahoon, come along after a break and he said, "You know Helena Murri?" "Ya." He says, "Well that's the gal your datin'."

I don't know we passed time a little bit there, but I got to know him pretty well. He was a good guy. He was just an old dirt farmer, but he had a lot of sense. Knew how to do things. That's part of the reason they had him there is to show them how to get that dirt off. All his life was hauling trucks, wagons with dump boards, tip the dump boards to get

---

[15] Helena M. Page

the dirt off and have to set it all back on. He was there kind of overseeing it. He let me know that I was going out with a relative.

I was concerned about how I would make a living, where we would live and if I was capable of supporting a wife.

"How did he propose? He asked me if I wanted to work in a "double-harness."

"We were engaged from Mar 1946 to Jul 1946. He took me to Logan after school to get the ring he had already picked out before I knew he was going to propose. As I was teaching school at that time. I remember that the students all wanted to see the ring when I got back to school."

(In Moms cedar chest is a picture cut out from a magazine of a man and woman kissing. Apparently, a student had cut it out and given it to Mom. They had written by the man, "Verl" and by the woman, "Miss Murri".)

"On a warm sunny summer day on 17 July 1946 we were married and sealed for time and all eternity in the newly constructed Idaho Falls temple."

"After we were through my dad had arranged to eat dinner in a hotel coffee shop. Probably the only place that had a restaurant in Idaho Falls back then. It was a hotel coffee shop the way that I remember. And that's where we had a dinner. His dad, Aunt Lexi's family, Aunt Ivy's family, my dad and mother were those who came to the dinner. That was our wedding dinner."[16]

After dinner, we took Dad's 1942 Plymouth and just took off, never told anybody we just took off. Left Dad there, he had to find a bus to get home. Anyway, when we got out of the temple she said something about she'd left a dress or something she wanted in Newdale so we drove back up there, (40 miles). When we came back down we couldn't find a hotel or a motel that we could get into.

Finally, we found a place in Idaho Falls that was just like an old barn. (**Grandma**: Junky). We decided we'd better take that 'cause it was getting late and so we stayed there that night; next morning we went up to Yellowstone Park. That's where we spent our honeymoon. We took a bedroll with us; we didn't have sleeping bags then. Well in the

---

[16] Helena M. Page

early morning there was a bear ran right on top of us. So we were awake early that morning.

Helena said, "We had a wonderful time in the park. First time neither one of us had ever been there. We stayed about 10 days on that trip. But he did get sick when we got into Jackson Hole. It must have been strep throat or something. He didn't get better from that until we got to Dayton and to a doctor. I don't know how he picked that up. Loaded up all my belongings in that 1942 Plymouth and drove down to Dayton. "

"We lived with his dad for, I can't tell you how long. (**Grandpa:** Not until Jean and Balls Kendall had moved out of the house that we'd bought.) "Verl told me then that he didn't want to milk cows, but as you know that is what happened for us to have a living on the land."[17]

My dad had a chance to buy a farm while I was in the service. He wrote to me and wanted to know if I was interested. I said yes, go ahead and buy it. So he bought it. That's the house he bought for us when we got married. The neighbor got married and he let him rent that until we got married and kicked them out, I guess. And then we moved into our first house. We lived in that house for 19 years, all of our children were born when we lived in that 4 room house.

"We bought another farm across the street. Then we moved into that other house. We lived in that house for 15 years and Brett said, about the time he was getting married, he

said, 'You need to build a new home.' After he got married, and because of the timing, it fit that way. So we mortgaged everything we owned and built our new home. It's on the same spot where we bought our first home. We just moved and cleaned all that out and built a home there. So that's no farther than we've moved in 57 years. Across the street and back. (**Grandpa**: We're still sleeping in the first bed that we bought. We got a new mattress and springs and stuff.) (**Grandma**: Bed frame, still the same. We're still using the chest of drawers he built. So we have a place to put our clothing in these sets of drawers. Verl built a crib for the babies. We still have the crib.)

---

[17] Helena M. Page

(**Grandpa**: Our furniture) (**Grandma**: Is old.)"[18] [Verl learned how to work with wood and was able to build much of the furniture that they needed. He built the kitchen cabinets, book shelves and more.]

The stove is still over there in the house it's the one that these people that was renting the house bought and put in there new. And when they got ready to move we talked them into selling us that one and they could get them another one. So, the stove was used when we got it, but we paid new price for it.

"Well, it had four rooms. It seemed like a real nice little home for two of us. Even though we had no bathroom, no central heating. But then I grew up with none of that anyway, so you didn't know. We were very happy, we had a nice little home. We were able to buy some new furniture. The table I still have and the bed Grandpa talked about earlier. Table and chairs and I like to keep a nice neat, clean home."

"I started teaching school right after we were married. Then I got pregnant soon after and so I quit teaching about the time they stopped the school for harvest vacation.

Though it's not really a vacation, they called it that. To harvest and work in the fields in the fall of the year, the beet fields and so that's when I quit teaching and a new teacher took my place. They wouldn't allow me to keep teaching when I was pregnant. It didn't happen in those days. Except for when my brother Herbert, died the fall of 1946, I guess we stayed home most of the time. We might have gone back to my mother's for Thanksgiving. Whenever we did in our early years of marriage it would take us about seven hours to drive from Dayton to Newdale where my parents lived. We had one cow, we lived on very little. It didn't take us a lot to live on, you know, there were two of us and we didn't have a lot of money and I don't know where we got our money. One cow I guess. That's all we had, tiny black cow. We milked her by hand."

---

[18] Helena M. Page

In the spring we lived on beet greens, then and that's what we had and a little bit of food that she had bottled. We had carrots of course that's in a tub of sand down in the basement.

Helena always raised a garden, and we had that to eat. She canned most of it. What we didn't eat was canned. Bottled I should say.

I guess we were poor, but we didn't know it. 'Cause most of the families around us were in the same category. Not only that, but most of the families were big families. Bishop, Bingham, Beutlers, all with 10 or more children, so we didn't, that's just something we was going to do, going to have some children, that's what you got married for and we accepted it. Now I wonder sometimes if the kids really felt good about it. 'Course, like I said, all of the families were big. I don't know any of the families that was less than four.

A lot of them were eight to twelve children. And that was just kind of the way we were raised. My dad and mother only had five kids. Of course the first one died as a baby so there was only four in there, but as brothers and sisters all but two of 'em had big families and their still, still united. When we have Page cousins' reunions, they support it. I guess that's kind of the way we was raised. We just think this is what we got married for and so we're going to raise a family. Not only that, on the farm with cows and crops, we had work for all of 'em. We'd have never made it through if we hadn't had, if the kids hadn't helped us. When we needed help they was there to do it.

"They do appreciate that they have learned how to work. And you hear this today in councel from our church leaders. 'Teach children how to work because they'll appreciate it in their later years.' So, I guess there are somethings we did do right as parents; we taught our children how to work. And we all worked together. We didn't just send somebody out to go do this job, hope they did it okay. Because we were right there with them to do it."

We worked as a family. We played as a family. Not very much playing, if you don't think so, ask them. But none the less, nearly all of 'em have come back and told us how much they appreciate that we taught them how to work. I remember when Clyde came back from his mission. This fellow (Marv) we was good friends, his folks had a steel fabricating place here in Salt Lake. When he got home, Clyde said something about he'd like to go down to Salt Lake and look for a job. I kinda hesitated a little bit. He said, "That's all right," he said, "There's no work down there. So let him go." So, we let him go, when he came back I think he had either three or four jobs. He was trying to run two of 'em. One guy said, "Hey, well pay for your folks to send your clothes and stuff that you want down here. You stay and work and we'll call them and have them send your things down."

Marv said, "Well, all that's happened, is you've taught those kids how to work and when these people see the kids know how to work, they won't let them get away from them if they can help it."

"If there's one thing you can say about the Page boys is pride in their work."[19]

A neighbor wanted to hire Clyde and I said, "No, I don't think so. When you put him on a job he stays with it until it's done. I'll never let him go."

But most part our kids was pretty diligent in what we asked them to do and how we asked them to do it. I was raised, that when you started a job, you finished it. Just like going out and trying to find some trouble, that's usually what happened, if you didn't stick with the job you were on. And if nothing else happened, then it was pleasant.

"I guess, because we've always worked so hard, after we once started having children, anytime there was any need for going to Preston, or later when we had chickens and we'd go up into Mink Creek to get saw dust from a saw mill to bed chickens, we would make that a special trip and have a picnic. We'd take a lunch so we could have a little picnic, stop along the side of the road and have lunch. We had four when we did that. When Janette was a baby we went up to north of Soda Springs, way out into the middle where there's nothing, we were searching for pasture for cattle. So we could haul cattle into that area to pasture them for the summer."

"One experience we had there were two different ones, but one was when, Grandpa Irvin said, 'Let's take some meat to make a dinner, cook it outside, build a fire and cook it." That was our plan, but time went on and on and on and on and we didn't stop we just kept searching for pasture couldn't find anything, and I was there in the car with four little children, trying to keep them contented, we finally drove to the nearest town which was another probably 15 to 20 miles I would guess from what I know today. And bought a can of tuna, we opened a can of  tuna, a can of pork and beans and that was our lunch. We didn't have to have a fire. And that's what we lived with that day for our picnic, so it was kind of like an adventure we

---

[19] Helena M. Page

thought we'd make it a fun one, but it didn't always turn out that way depending on what had to happen."

"Another trip we took when Brett was a baby, well he was old enough to walk. He was little, and they were hauling cattle. This time they had the truck loaded with cattle. We had a flat tire on the big truck. Irvin and Verl went back to town to get that fixed. I took the two kids up on the side hill. We wandered around along the early wild flowers and sage brush and that sort of thing until, we finally got it fixed, traveled clear up into Soda Springs, in the mountains had one flat tire and were able to fix it there. While we waited for that we were just swamped with misquotes. And poor Janette, just like she had honey on her or something. Oh, they liked her, they really did. But we had to wait and sit in the truck all this time while they were fixing the truck so we could go on and two loads of cattle. We always had two vehicles. That was a safety thing too. To have more than one vehicle when you were out in the middle of the mountains and a long way away from anybody."

"Another trip or adventure we had, I call it adventure, memorable not humorous exactly  was when he came in one morning and said we're going over to Bear Lake to find a big pole to put out on the derrick. They had a saw mill over there where you could get these big boom poles that would be heavy enough for the derrick. My mother was living with us. So, we took the ice chest, filled it with a picnic and took that with us. We went over there for what he needed and made a picnic out of it. And that was kind of the things we did that was adventures and trips that we wouldn't have done otherwise."[20]

I guess when we went up there huntin' for pasture. Helena told part of it. I had a cousin that lived in Grace, named Ruby. We stopped and asked her and her husband where the different people were that had pasture. We took off early, thinking we were going to find a pasture and get back home. We went two places where they told us to go and they didn't have any room for pasture. We finally found a pasture and it was getting late we were back home and the next day we looked again. Like she said, we'd take the big truck a load of cattle and then the pickup. I don't know, we hauled the cattle on the pick up and went back to town to get the tire fixed. We should have hauled the cattle out of it. But probably the best experience where  we were up there getting the cattle and this fellow had a cattle in his pasture and when

---

[20] Helena M. Page

 his horse went down in the slough there to find some more cattle. He got out of it but his horse wasn't too hot. When the saddle broke, the cinch broke and it dumped him out there in the middle of that slough with that saddle. He packed that out again. He was about give out by the time we were through. We got all of the cattle out. It was after dark by the time we left. But this one time the Ford pickup, it wasn't running very good. So I told Dad to stay behind me with the truck so that if something happened, he would get me. We got clear down to Cleveland and I couldn't see them. I wondered what had happened to them. Instead of being smart and pulling off the side of the road, I drove down into a drive way. Just got turned around my lights shining back up on the highway and here they both was in back. As luck would have it the truck didn't die, it kept going. The problem we were having with it, I don't know if it wasn't getting enough gas or what. But you'd drive along and all of the sudden she'd just die out. I lucked out that time. Man that was a long ways to haul them cows back then before the roads were straight. Well part of the road was just two tracks, grass and weeds growing up in the middle of it. It was out in the wilderness. But it was good pasture once we got 'em up in there.

"In 1950, in order to provide for the family of seven children and feed for increased cow herd, Verl worked for Lyman Balls to pay off a mortgage on 20 acres of land, as it took more land to produce feed for the increased cattle herd. In 1965, we purchased 40 acres of land from Orson Nelson of the former Arnold Naef Farm and moved into the house on that land, living there for 15 years. In 1979, we had a new home built on the plot of land where we began our married life."

"Verl worked with his father on both of their farms for about 30 years as it was necessary to use the same equipment. Farming practices were in transition in the late 1940s from horses to mechanized farming. Verl's first tractor was a Farmall, a cultivision tractor. Helena learned to drive it attached to the derrick cable for 'putting up hay.' Verl taught his children to work together as a family in the beet, potato, hay and grain fields, teaching the children that when you start a job, you finish it."

"Verl enjoyed rodeo, so all the family attended the rodeo each year at the Preston Night rodeo the end of Jul. for recreation. He supported the extended Page families, making sure the family could attend the annual family reunion each year. In 1976, Verl and Helena began their own family reunion, which is still on-going, looked forward to and enjoyed by all who can attend."

"Verl loved to travel, so for weddings, funerals, baptisms, or special programs, he would arrange his work so they would have an opportunity to travel. In 1996, for our 50th anniversary our children arranged and paid for a Church History Tour through four states, visiting church history sites in Missouri, Iowa, Nebraska, and Illinois. We have attended Barbershop Competitions with our son, Clyde and family, in South Dakota, Tennessee, Oregon, and Salt Lake City. We have been able to attend temples in Arizona, California on trips with family and for weddings. We have traveled in 24 of the lower 48 states."

"Verl served on the Dayton Cemetery Board with Carl Bingham and Perry Phillips for about 30 years, part of those years as Chairman. He donated many hours and the use of his truck in that service. He has served faithfully in the church his entire life in Dayton and Clifton First wards. He became a member of Clifton First ward in Jan. 1981."[21]

Verl's Diary Entries

Nov. 22, 1971

We have had extremely wet weather for the last two years. We have had good crops while Clyde and Marva were and are on their missions.

We have topped our beet each fall by hand until this year and we still haven't got them out. We had an enjoyable trip out to Mountain Home to see Maurice and his family this summer. On the way home we went to Rexburg and brought Janette home for a short

visit. She has worked up there all summer. Clyde came home the last of Jun. and worked here for about two months, then went to Salt Lake City and got a job in a warehouse and started night school. He spent 2 years in the Florida mission. While he was on his mission, Bishop Philips asked me to be Superintendent of the Dayton ward Sunday school. Also now I am on the finance committee to raise funds to build 5 classrooms and a library on the chapel.

---

[21] Helena M. Page

Dec. 4, 1972

We have had a real busy year. Marva has Cushing' disease and has been in the hospital in Salt Lake City for weeks and we have had to take her back to SL several times. We bought a new 1972 Pontiac car so we could make the trips. We have had good crops this year. Marva completed her Cumorah mission before she got sick. We built a milk house and are building a cow shed. We have poured more than 50 yards of cement in the corrals. Dad  comes over and helps me a lot. He is 75 years old. I am still on the finance committee and we have the class rooms nearly done. I'm still president of the Sunday school and still have the same counselors. I am also on the cemetery board. Shalene is in Virginia, Marva here with us and under doctor's care, Clyde just graduated from computer school and is working in Salt Lake City. Janette is in school in Logan. Brett is a senior. Verna is a Jr and Kelly in 6th grade.

Dec. 31, 1973

Our hay and grain crops were not very good and hay is $55.00 a ton, Barley is $100.00 a ton. We had a good corn crop. It was wet and we broke down a lot while harvesting it. Helena drove truck for us. We finished the cow shed enough to get the cows in it in Nov. We poured the south wall on the corn silo and some in the corral and the alley in the shed. We didn't raise any beets this year and beet pulp cost $100.00 a ton. Brett started to Ricks College and seems to enjoy it. Janette is in the mission training school at Provo  learning Spanish. She is going to Uruguay – Paraguay. I was released as Sunday school president in Dec. Marva is in Logan and works in Lewiston. Clyde lives in Dallas Texas and loves his work there. He and Dixie were married in Apr. 26, 1973. Shalene and Ron moved to IL. I had a cow catch me in the middle of the field and tromp me real good. I was released from the finance committee. We have had Grandma Murri here with us this summer. She had her 80th birthday while she was here. She is in Arizona now. Helena has a job 3 days a week working in the grade school library as media specialist. We bought a pipeline milker (zero) and a bulk milk tank (510 gal). We are sending about 1000 lbs. of milk a day. Prices for everything has really jumped. Twine $24.30 a bale.

Nov. 10, 1975

It seems like time really flies by. Missed last year somehow. I have just been put in as secretary of the Sunday school. We have had Janette home with us since she finished her mission. She is planning to marry Knute Lund Dec. 12, 1975. We are still milking between 35 and 40 cows. The growing season was real short this year. Our crops are about average this year. We bought a new "David Brown Tractor and loader last fall and a new, New Holland baler this fall. Shalene and Ron came out from Illinois in June they have a baby boy named Paul Mark, born 1 Jan. 1975. Clyde and Dixie were here the same time with Nathan born 12 Mar. 1974, and was here again to help with the corn the last of Sept. Marva married Ned Packer Apr. 25, 1974. They live in Salt

Lake City. Sterling was born to them 10 Feb 1975. So we now have three grandsons and all of them were here in June. We remodeled the kitchen this summer. Brett went to the Kentucky mission Nov. 2, 1974. They divided the mission and he is in the Tennessee mission. Kelly and Verna are in high school. Grandpa Page has built three cattle mangers for me this fall. He still likes to do a few things and comes over every few days. He is 78 years old.

Jan 3, 1977

We had an unusual spring as we got our crops in fairly early. Dad came over and drove

tractor for me. Then on the 12 of May he had a severe heart attack and was in the hospital for several weeks. He is home now but can't do anything. Kelly went to California for 10 days with the explorers. We got a frost on the 15th of June and froze the corn to the ground. It got green and looked good when it froze again on 30 of June. Then froze again the end of Aug. So we had a real light corn crop. Our wheat and barley were real good this year. Bill Ward, Eileen and his sister Dorothy came from California to see us one day. Brett got home from his mission on Nov. 6 and we had all the family here but

Shalene, Ron and Paul. Helena and I went to Manti, Saint George and Mesa Temples, visited with Rhonda Lou, Mary Lou, Vera and family and in Dallas with Clyde and family. We came home for Christmas and then went with Lyn and Hilda to Los Angeles and stayed with Del and Esther. Ina Mae came and we went to San Diego for Cyril Murri's funeral. Helena's brother and sister were all there except for Leda. Brett has gone to BYU to school so Kelly, Verna and I are milking 41 cows now. Clyde and Dixie have a new son named Keith Owen born Aug. 5, 1976. Janette and Knute have a son Layne born 28 Aug. - Makes 5 grandsons for us. We held our first family reunion on Jul. 24 with all but Ron, Brett and Clyde and family.

30 Dec. 1977

We didn't get any storm all winter and had a dry spring. We had 1/3 the normal turn water, with no 5 mile water so had to buy pumps and sprinkler to stretch our water. We had good crops considering how short of water we were. Rene Johnson, Veldoy Martin and I put a pipe line from the west canal to our [field], but run out of water before we got it completed. We couldn't get our corn chopped so purchased corn chopper this fall. Brett and  Rosaline Shepherd got married in the Provo Temple 23 Jun. 1977. Brett helps us and we are milking 50 cows now. We have had a stormy wet fall which makes it bad for feeding and milking, but we need the moisture.

On Jul. 17, 1946 I married Helena Murri of Newdale, [in the Idaho Falls Temple]. Helena was a school teacher, [in the Dayton Elementary School.] I have lived in Dayton all of my life and my occupation is farming. I farm 40 acres and I am leasing 40 acres. In church work, I am the Aaronic Priesthood General Secretary and the Ward Teacher district supervisor. I am a seventy also.

I have three sons and four daughters of which I am proud.

"Though he is quiet, he has a great sense of humor and loves to hold my (Helena's) hand."[22]

2000

I would like to begin with a story about my Uncle Dick McCombs, my mother's brother. He went to California, San Francisco area to work. He would never write home to his mother, my Grandma McCombs. But every spring, he would have a produce company send a box of asparagus to his mother. She would share the asparagus with all her families in this area. Grandma said, "Well, we know that he is still alive."

We had asparagus for Sunday dinner and it reminded me of this story. Today we don't need asparagus for our families to keep in contact with us and each other. We have our families get together for blessings, baptisms, ordinations, missionaries and awards. These events have helped our relationship and relationships with our children. I appreciate how Mom has kept the families together with letters, phone calls, now e-mail.

If you want to know more about me, read the Mar. 2000 Readers Digest, P. 92 "When you're too shy." It reminded me of my mother, Lareta who went to M.I.A only after her friend offered to give a prayer if she, Lareta, would have been called on to do so.

---

[22] Helena M. Page

Having your mother help me, I have been able to fulfill my church callings. I am sure I married the right person who has encouraged me to do things that have been difficult to do. We have had a good relationship thru the difficult times and the good times because we worked together.

Family

My grand folks did family get togethers. I guess you may not have noticed. Now when we have a returned missionary or something like that. Notice how much the family gets together, just like it is around here like the snow kinda backs some of them down. But we still had quite a few of the family. Especially when these missionaries return. We've had enough of them return.  I guess you call it tradition when we support them when they go on missions. So I guess we've done a few things right or the family wouldn't have kept supporting us in it. But it's a little like this friend of mine. He has one boy and one girl. I think he's only got one grandson. That's all I know about anyway. In fact, he likes to come to our reunions. When he's up there, one time I was talking to him and sitting around the crowd and he's says, "You sure got a lot of them here." He said, "I got one grandson and he don't know who I am." They raised him in the city. He didn't have work like we had. Our family learned to work together. I know that when we went to go somewhere they were all in the car and ready to go. There wasn't a lot of fighting and bickering. In that we've been real fortunate in that our family is, when somebody decides to do something, the family gets behind them real quick, instead of draggin' feet. So along with all of the mistakes we've made, we've made a few good things in our life.

"I think he had a talent for teaching his children how to work. I think there's a talent to that. I think there's a talent in learning how to get children to work and how to work with children and family so that you'll work together."[23]

Well, you have to be consistent with it. I know some would say, "You can't do that." And expect them to know what they were doing. I always figured when you told them something, if you told them you'd knock their head off, you'd better go knock it off. I kinda stuck to that with the children, when I told them to do something, that's what I wanted done. For the most part they've been easy to teach what to do what you ask. The trouble I see now days, I see a lot of them, whose kids will climb up on the chair aside of his dad or on a the sofa, and start after the kid has to take him off set him down here, pretty soon the kids right back up there. He never taught him that he isn't supposed to

---

[23] Helena M. Page

do it he just set him down. That works but, it worked for me to tell them no, that it wasn't to do anymore. So, I guess it was a good thing, I hope. I'm sure pleased with the way the kids have turned out. I had one of the kids kind scold me because we worked him too hard. Pretty good and after he got through I said, "Now you just set here a minute and think about it. How many people do you know with families like ours that doesn't have a kid that's been stealing, a jail bird or into mischief somewhere?" I said, "Now we look back at what we done with our family. Yes, we've been real fortunate." In fact, the kids have picked up spouses that kinda went along with what we did. But our kids, I guess their mother taught em the right and the wrong way because we never had any trouble with a drug problem. We're getting this too long for you, so I'd better stop.

"Probably our greatest accomplishment or joy has been having our children. Raising and having family I think as we're taught in the church. Families are so much more important. I mean there's a lot more stress on that as we hear it today. Although it has always been important in our lives. I think to work together as we've talked a lot about in this interview. That each one, we all worked together so that when Clyde, who was the first to go on a mission, there was money there to pay for that mission. And each one that came along that happened again. They all supported the one that had to leave to go on a mission and money was saved for that purpose. And we were truly blessed. I can't express how blessed we've been. On the small farm we had and the small herd of cows we had enough money to support missionaries and two at the same time. It isn't the same cost that it is today, but in relation to the values of money then today, it was just as difficult then to support missionaries. And we were able to do it. And I believe that that was probably our biggest accomplishment overall has been having missionaries in our family. Because not every family does that, they might be lucky to have one."

"We had girls that said, "We want to serve a mission." And so we encouraged them. And what experience we had with that, just to give you an idea how we had to work together to accomplish this, was one of them was at school, trying to go to school or babysitting or working and she said I want to go on a mission. I said, "Well you must move home and help do something at home to earn money, to save money for other things so we don't have to hire anybody. You do the work then we'll have the money to send you on a mission." And she did it and she went on a mission. And that's the way we had to do this to, because I feel like in my heart the greatest accomplishment as a family is having our three sons and three daughters serve missions. And you can tell it's a blessing in our lives now."

"They can't ignore that, even though there may be other things come up in their life that aren't quite like we think they ought to be, I still believe deep down in their hearts, having that mission has been a blessing for them. You hear that as missionaries report from their missions. How much they have grown from that experience, they can't deny that. " [24]

The thing that I'm most impressed with is our families going on missions and the younger ones helping support them. Then when they come back they help support the ones younger. Which we probably couldn't have done alone without the kids to help us. They might be out on their own, but still, when the younger ones went on missions they sent money to us or put it in the bank for them so that those kids were each able to go on a mission. They'd helped with the older ones, so they didn't feel like they were sponging on them. The older ones felt obligated to help support them. That's a feeling that a lot of parents don't instill in their children is to support one another. What's mine is mine and what's yours is mine if I can get it. We see a lot of that now. But back when we were raising kids, 'course we had one advantage, most of the neighbors were just like we were. And their families were helping them to support their missionaries so it wasn't something that was different from those around us. It's been real interesting in our married life, how the kids have conducted themselves. And now even the grandkids, I feel like all that I know about them still active in the church and feel like they're obligated to help the rest of the families to do those things that are necessary in the church. I don't know, I've made a lot of mistakes, but the Lord blessed me with a few and that's one of the things that's turned out right.

---

[24] Interview with Elizabeth Page, 2006

Spiritual Experiences

"Well, I think we had a really spiritual feeling within our family when Bryce died. That was a real traumatic experience for us. I felt it more than when my own brother and father died and my mother. I don't know maybe because we were just a little closer to the family, even though we had other deaths that usually brings spirituality within your family. That was real hard on Brett's family when they lost Bryce by drowning. And they'd been to the temple. Doing what they were supposed to do that day, and they came home and the baby missing."

We were out trying to find him, searching for him.

"I still think there was a bonding, a spirituality there within our family at that time bringing our family together."

"One is when Shalene called me and told me she had cancer. And she told me after I had spent a lot of hours with her on the telephone. That first month, in Dec. 2002, a year ago now, we had linked to a free phone call situation I can't explain that, I don't know it all. But I was able to talk to her every day. To see how she was feeling, what her feelings were and share my feelings with her. After that it was every other day or every two days and I did that for months. And when I see how strong she has been and staying close to the church, not letting this break up their marriage as you hear it happening in people's lives when there's a terrible illness. They struggled, both of them, with their health and trying to overcome the problems with their health. I felt like this has brought me closer together specifically with her because of that situation. But it has also tied our family closer together, because we'd say, Janette, you put her name in the temple in Idaho Falls, Verna, you call Jordan River Temple, put their family names, not just hers but Ron or others if they felt the desire to. We did it in Logan, we did it in numerous temples. Shalene told me later, she felt that, she felt the spirituality that came from all of the family supporting her. We felt it within our whole family. I know that it's been a highly, extremely, spiritual experience in our family. We hope we have that closeness when other traumatic experiences happen in life, we'll do that again. You know, but we still know it, because we've all tried to stay close to the church, we've tried to use fasting and prayers, and temple work and obedient to go to the temple, put the names in the temple that has all helped to make that all very spiritual."

It's was quite a shock to me when Brett said he had cancer. I had a hard time to deal with that. He's due to go have the doctors check him up again now. He's got to find time, but with this change in jobs it's kinda hauled him out. He needs to check up on that. He had this melanoma cancer. That stuff spreads real fast, they got that checked last time he was up there and said it was all out, he wouldn't have to come up for a year. Farming with him, we used the same equipment, and worked together whether it was hauling hay or whatever we had to do we worked together. That kinda hit me real hard because, what am I going to do? I can't run his place and mine too, because he's a hard worker. He got overhauled, he still does.

These things worked out, and I'm sure that we've been blessed maybe for what we've done, even if it wasn't enough, it's as much as it ought to have been. It's real interesting how much we can be blessed even if we're not doing all of the things we're supposed to do. I guess it's a good thing. I am concerned about whether I've been good enough for the wife and mother of my children. To me she's worthy. I get awful, awful tearing when I talk about this. It's all I pray to know, I appreciate what your mother (your grandmother) puts up just to live with this old guy; A lot of it has been through our church activities and stuff. I'm sure that's what's helped. It's helped us a lot in raising our family. And I think it's helped with kids a lot to know that their folks still know what the church is all about.

There is one other thing I wouldn't mind ya havin'. There's been two times that's been, rough, I've lost count. That was when I lost my father, I'd worked with him all my life. Been a little hard to think, that I gotta do now without him tellin' what to do, of course not now, but back when he died.

Then when my brother got killed. We were waiting for him, he was going to come out from Preston and pour some cement. He was going to pour some cement with Dad, in Dad's shop. Anyway, when he didn't come we got concerned about him and so we got in the car, we was all ready to go. He had been in the lumber yard and loaded up on 50 bags of cement to mix up for pour. When they loaded that, they loaded it right on the back of the trailer. The trailer was hooked up on the Allis Chalmers tractor.

And he started on that Preston hill, the load from on the back had been flipped on the hitch of the tractor and tipped over.

We know the tractor had been on its side, now nobody was there to witness any of this. We knew that he had been on the tractor and fell off. The tractor had come loose from the trailer and that's when the tractor came off the trailer hitch went in the air, so the back end of the trailer just fell down to the ground. And I know that he went under that trailer when it took off the side of the road. And his body was laying on the road, on the shoulder of the road on one side and the tractor up on the other side, sitting right side. Nobody had seen it, but somebody had been there, we know that. When we got over there nobody seemed to know anything; we finally went over and picked up his wife.

This was my dad and I, we went over to pick up his wife, at their home. We asked her where he was, she said, oh he's out to Dayton. Well we knew he wasn't, we went over to the car and went back to where Keith had got killed.   There wasn't anybody that knew anything, so we went up to the hospital; no they didn't know anything, went over to the clinic, they didn't know anything. And finally we couldn't find out anything so we went back out to where he'd died. And his Bishop had come in there just after we got there we saw him and this Bishop came off to the side, he said didn't you know that Keith has been killed. I said, "No, we don't." He said, "Well, he was killed in that accident." And I said, "Will you come over to Dayton and tell my dad and his wife about it?" He said, "I can't." So I got in the car and drove back into town to the court house like I dared tell him. And I told him.

Anyway, but I think that's one of the hardest things I ever had to do, and it still bothers me just to talk about it. But, anyway, when we got there, everywhere we'd go nobody knew anything about it. But everybody knew about it, even Grandma had found out about it. Before we did, cause some of the neighbors out there had heard about it. And she'd happened to be at the Dayton store where they were talking about it. But I guess we finally went to the mortuary. I remember the mortician was a good friend of the family and Uncle Joe Bodily came there. Now this is after they'd got him (Keith) in there and start to clean him up, and they had him back in the room there they'd wash him up and when we got in there the mortician, Dad said he want to see Keith. He says, "We don't let anybody back in there." Dad just turned to him and said, "It's my son, I wanna see him; If you want to take me back there alright; If not, I'm going in anyway." So the four of us went back in there. He was on a marble slab, they had washed him up. He had broke up, banged pretty bad, legs broke, ribs, arm but anyway when we came back out of there I wondered why dad wanted to see that. I know now that he wanted to know how bad he had suffered. But it was something I'll bet very, very few people ever see something like that after an accident. They might see it at the accident, but after they take the body and clean it up. But that mortician, he was determined we wasn't going to see, and my dad was just as determined that he was.

I'm happy that he did, it still wasn't a very pretty experience. Something that kinda, well it still haunts me about it, go in there Keith was always a joking, and we get in there and touch him and it's about touching oh anything with no life in it. It's like touching that desk there I had never felt that until I touched him. Course I felt the same thing when your mother (Dixie) passed away. I reached in and took hold of her hand and wrist to see if I, more or less confirm what I knew from Keith. What it's like, there's no life there. It's just like a piece of wood or rock or something, there's just no life there, but you can feel that when you touch it. I don't know if you touched your mother (Dixie) when she passed away but I did and I should apologize to you for doing it, but I just had to know. But some of the more unpleasant things that we go through too, that I probably shouldn't have bothered you with. Felt like maybe it wouldn't hurt for you to know about it. Least if one knew about it, but back into the strong family that we have we manage to get through.

We get teary sometimes, we get kinda despondent and discouraged after it's all said and done these things are a kind of a testimony, a test to see whether we are really, really interested in what we're supposed to be learning. And I know the gospel is true just about, but not as good as I ought to. But that don't mean you can't, it's somethin' that we learn through our life experiences. I better be through, I get too teary.

"Being able to do genealogy has built my testimony. It's probably been the strongest part of my testimony, working in family history. I know that, I guess I got the feeling of wanting to do that when I still had children at home and took my first genealogy class. About 50 years ago. It stayed with me all the rest of my life. And so I know it's important to me and I know it has built my testimony and I really appreciate that and I'm grateful for it."

"Verl retired at age 80 following hip surgery and selling the cow herd after 60 years of dairying. In 2012 Verl lived in the Heritage Home for a month and a half. Following an illness in Aug. 2012, he lived in The Franklin County Transition Care Center. Helena lived at home in Dayton."[25]

"Some of Clyde's families more recent, fondest memories was when we were able to take him out of the Care Center for Family Reunions and one year we arranged to have him brought home to see the corn harvest. He enjoyed being there, watching out the window as the trucks came in and out. Although we know he wanted to be out there working too!"

"One of our fondest memories, is having Dad and Mom come to our home for Thanksgiving just a few months before he died. We put our Christmas tree up early so that he could enjoy that weekend with us and feel the joys of the season in a home, not just the care center."

"He was so grateful and so happy all week end. It was hard to take him back. He didn't want to go, but he understood that we could not care for him in our home, with his special needs. He passed away less than two months later."[26]

---

[25] Helena M. Page
[26] Terri N. Page

"Now in our ninetieth years of life and 68 years of marriage, we are blessed with Seven children and spouses, 39 grandchildren and spouses, and 77 great grandchildren as of this date. I know that Verl has a testimony of the gospel although he can't express it. He has been faithful in this church callings and attended church where he lived and I attended church in the Clifton First ward almost every Sunday. My testimony has grown immensely as I now live alone and spend days with Verl at the Center, knowing that we will be together forever in the eternities as a family. We are thankful for our families and we know that the Church of Jesus Christ of Latter-day Saints is true."

"Verl passed away in the care center, in Preston, Idaho on Jan. 14, 2015, at 10:30 am. His funeral was held on Jan. 19, 2015 at the Clifton First Ward Chapel, in Clifton, Idaho. Many of his posterity, along with other extended family members and friends were there to show their respect and love for him. He was buried in the Dayton City Cemetery, Dayton, Idaho."[27]

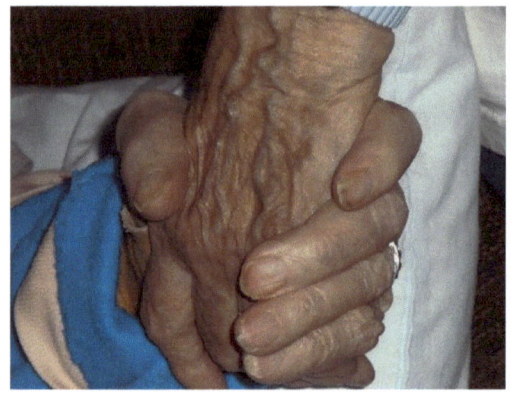

---

[27] Helena M. Page

Memories of Dad, Grandpa, Great Grandpa

Dad

What about the rooster that would chase us all over the back yard? We weren't bothering

him, just taking the eggs from the hens. From the noise of the roosters, you would have thought the rooster was giving up something. Later he did. Yum, yum.

The spring time was planting potato time – but first we would cut the potatoes so every piece had one eye. Memorial day morning was time to cut potatoes and begin planting. Then when school was out, thinning sugar beets and tending them for the summer was a full time job. Grandpa Page would tell us to finish so we could go for a ride. What a wonderful way to end the day. Thanks Dad, for a great lesson in learning to work. Even when the job was thought to be too hard, there was the thought of school and a day of reunions to relish the quiet times.

Many thanks, Dad.

Love,

Shalene

Dear Grandpa,

Happy Birthday. I wish you the very best with many more to come.

I remember the times when you would hook an old car hood to the tractor and lock the cuter brakes and whip us around the fields.

I mostly appreciated all the times that you and Grandma would always come for those family activities, you showed me that there is nothing more important than family.

Your work ethic is like no other. In all the jobs that I've had I've never had one as difficult as yours seemed to be, yet I've probably never received or experienced the satisfaction that you have by growing something from nothing.

You're my Grandpa, a man of great strength and great faith.

Love,

Paul

Dear Grandpa,

I have lots of memories of you and the farm. I want to thank you for baptizing me and making time to come down and support me in the various things I do. I remember you and Grandma coming down for various concerts, graduation and my farewell and welcome home. With so many grandchildren you still know us individually.

Your such a hard worker and I really admire that. I hope that I marry a man with some of those qualities you have. Hard worker, a strong testimony and still so in love with Grandma, 50+ years. You definitely deserve those naps on the kitchen floor.

I love you and wish you many more happy birthdays,

Love,

Tiffany

Grandpa,

I can remember when you baptized me, what an awesome experience that was for me. I can remember when I was in primary, you and Grandma came to a grandparent's night. I appreciate the willingness that you and Grandma had to come to the little activity that meant so much.

How you traveled two hours to come and stay for only a short time.

Thank you for the many memories that you and I have made.

Love always and forever,

Nicole

Grandpa…

It's always been fun coming up here to visit. I remember the times when we would go out on the tractors or I would just tag along with you. It's been fun to see you with your cattle out milkin bright and early and I would walk out and watch.

The times when you would come out and be there for all the special occasions like my baptism, blessings and all the other times you would just come and visit.

Thanks for all the moral support

Love you tons,

Dave

What I love about Grandpa is that he never gave up on something that he loves. People would say that he should sell his farm, but he never did.

Another thing that I love about Grandpa is his love for animals.

I want to remember how much he cared for animals and loved them too.

I remember one time when I stayed up at Grandma and Grandpa's house and I wanted to help milk the cows and whenever I made a mistake Grandpa never got mad at me.

He always wants to be a part of everything and everyone s lives,

I love you Grandpa Page!!

Love,

Melissa

Dad,

As I have thought about growing up and some of the activities in which we participated, one of the foremost that I can remember is Dad using a sawed off baseball bat or an axe handle and hitting a tennis ball to have us catch. Typically he would be up close to the house and us kids would be near the barn or haystack trying to catch his fly balls.

I don't suppose I will ever forget the Christmas holidays in which Marvin Gerstner and 6 or so priests came up from Salt Lake to spend time with us. I remember well Dad taking the time to hook up a hood to the tractor and probably burning out the brakes spinning us in circles out in the field. I don't think those young men had ever done anything like that before in their lives!! There were many winter times we would "hood ride" mostly in the yard – nonetheless, it was exciting.

I suppose the most important thing Dad taught us kids was how to work hard. I well remember many of his quotations: "You're slower than cold tar," "Get a move on it," among others

I remember well the summer you helped Ted Murdock with his farm work. I remember helping you haul hay and take care of his grain. You never complained about the time it took you away from our own harvest.

I also remember you permitting me to use the truck and drive it to help Perry Phillips harvest his dry farm grain. I had sheared a pin in the transmission but there was no complaining or criticism about how it may have interfered with our farm work.

Although you may have had long lists of things to do, you were always willing to help the neighbors.

I also remember visiting your home teaching families and taking chunks of cheese at Christmas time.

Marva

To my father-in-law,

I have enjoyed many times here on the farm when we've visited. Thank you for putting up with me. I appreciate your help on some of my home projects and for your good example to me and my children.

You've raised a wonderful daughter who has been a very good mother to our children. You've taught her some good principles which she has passed on to our children.

I only regret that I couldn't be of more help to you. I hope I've been able to help in some small way on projects here on the farm.

I can honestly say that I've enjoyed being here at the farm and associating with you and your family just as much as with my own parents and brothers and sisters.

And I also hope that I can enjoy many more visits with you in the future.

Love,

Your son-in-law,

Ned

To my Grandpa,

I have many memories of you!! Some of my favorite memories include riding on the motorcycle with Tiffany and holding on for dear life through the corn rows. It was neat watching the water rush through the rows.

I also remember coming back into the house and hearing before seeing you sleeping on the floor in the living room. You work so hard and deserve a good nap!

Wishing you many more happy years,

Love always,

Hillary

Dear Grandpa,

It's hard to come up with just a couple of memories. I feel like I grew up on "Grandpa's farm". I definitely learned many lessons on the farm that taught me how to work hard and never give up. I have been successful because of all those summers I spent working with you.

I will never forget feeding calves, riding motorcycles, driving a tractor when I was 6, throwing cats out of the barn, hood rides, watching trains go by, big family reunions, the hat collection, and the time you stayed up waiting for me to get back from a date when it got foggy.

I will always cherish these memories and many more that I get to relive whenever I visit. We will always go out of our way to visit. When we have kids, we will make sure that they know all about "Grandpa's farm."

Oh, you're right Grandpa, sometimes the best place to sleep is right in the middle of the floor!

Sterling

Grandpa,

I haven't been part of the family for too long, but I've had a glance at your life.

You are a strong man both physically and spiritually. You have taught your children the gospel and the meaning of work.

In the short time I've been a part of the family, I see the respect that everyone has for you. You are a great man. I admire you strength and determination in running the farm. I would have thrown my hands in the air long before. Your health isn't perfect yet you continue to push forward. Your determination inspires your children and grandchildren. I know Sterling received the great blessing of determination from you. He too will not give up.

We love you very much and wish you all the joy life can bring. You deserve the best that life has to offer. I know that your life has been very blessed and that our Heaven Father keeps a close watch over you.

Love,

Staci

November 2000

Dad,

Just wanted to express some thought to you about you on your birthday. You have always been a great Dad. You have always set a great example for me in honesty, integrity and righteous living.

You taught me that I should do everything that I could to make Sunday a Sabbath day and not a day to work. I remember that you would save the long running water sets for Sunday so that you didn't have to spend so much time irrigating. You could have used them at night so that you could get more sleep. You know, you never asked me to do anything other than milking and feeding on Sunday. In fact we used to load the corn silage up on Saturday so that it would require less work on Sunday. What a great example of keeping the Sabbath day holy!

I remember going and playing with friends on the stockyards on Sunday. I don't remember how you felt about that, but I understand now that it wasn't in harmony with the Sabbath.

You obviously have good taste, because you picked a wonderful wife. She has supported you and filled the areas that you needed as you have improved yourself over the years.

You have been a great example of hard work. I remember one fall during the potato harvest, it was raining and you slipped on the mud on the tractor and poked the handle on the hitch in your ribs and broke three ribs. You never even stopped to rest but kept on working, bucking spuds, until the harvest was complete. You then went to work harvesting the sugar beets. I don't remember how the weather was the remaining of the harvest, but I do remember that by Christmas, you had pneumonia and could hardly get out of bed. Every time you coughed it would jar those broken ribs.

Thank you for setting such a great example in every way, especially honesty, hard work, fairness, obedience and love.

Love,

Clyde

Dad,

When I think of you, I first see a man of quiet strength, wisdom and patience.

You have given great advice and support from day one and I really appreciate it!

I really enjoy it when you can travel with our family. I will always remember out trip to Spokane. That's when I discovered how much Clyde takes after you.

Dad (Verl) loved to travel! He enjoyed going on drives in Idaho, taking new roads and just seeing the beautiful fields, meadows, mountains and valleys.

As we drove throughout the country, Clyde would discuss with Dad the crops that were growing there and how they most likely would irrigate them. As we drove around, I learned a lot about farming and what different crops looked like and how hard they are to plant, harvest and sell. Those conversations were very enjoyable to me. We loved to have Dad and Mom travel with us. If we gave them our route, Mom would look up highlights along the way and we often felt like we had our own personal travel guide.

I know that as a family and personally we have drawn on your strength a lot and I am grateful that we have such a great man to teach us. I think that the first time I began to understand a little about farming, was one day as we were in your home and you offered the family prayer. You did just as we are taught in the Book of Mormon. You prayed over your fields, and crop, your

cows, your family, everything that you had stewardship over. Your prayers have always touched me. I knew that you loved and depended on that Divine assistance. This and other experiences, showed me how you humbly prayed for the blessings you desired and then got up and worked so hard.

Thank you for all you do! I love you.

Love,

Terri

Grandpa,

After spending years in school, learning about high tech stuff and how the "newest" idea is going to change the world, I can't help but think of the more simple truth's that you taught me in just a couple of summers on the farm.

Work is a given, but it wasn't just work. I was working with what comes naturally, working with nature and working with God. It reminds me of a statement Abby (from the Dear Abby Column) made to "Use common horse sense, which can be found in the stable mind." Grandpa I'm sure she was talking about you.

Thanks for teaching me more on how to change the world in a couple of summers than years of college has.

Nathan

Memories of Grandpa, 23 Nov. 2000

Hola Abuelitos!

I don't know that I have had any huge life changing experiencing with grandpa. I do know that I have had many little life influencing moments. I love the little things that he says to make us laugh. Like when he steps on my feet and says, "Well, you walk on them don't you? Why can't I?" Or when no matter what time of the morning you wake up he is already out and about and says "Up for all day or just the rest of it?" All my years of visiting, I don't think that on one occasion I have been up before him. He has taught me the importance of work ethic, which I also believe he passed on to my Dad who has influenced me the same way. I don't know to this day that I could keep up with him one day on the farm. He also manages to enjoy his free time. I have seen him sit for hours enjoying the company of his children and family, even during the busiest of seasons of farm life. He has always managed to take time out for his family. This is obvious by the love he receives from his family today. In a world where the family is falling apart, Grandpa has maintained his family together (I am sure with much help from Grandma, but she will have to be patient, her day will come.

On a day of thanks, I am grateful for a Grandpa who is really interested in his family, a true example and hero. Hope you have a great birthday Grandpa. Sorry I couldn't be there, but I am sure I will see you soon to tell you in person.

Love ya,

Keith

Matthew stayed and worked on the farm so that Grandpa and Grandma could go on their church history tour. After they returned, Grandpa and Matthew were in the barn. Grandpa told Matthew that the church was true. He bore his testimony to Matthew and it helped strengthen Matthew's testimony of the Gospel.

Grandpa

I love the ways your eyes light up when you smile!

You have a wonderful sense of humor!

I loved it when you gave me whisker kisses! ☺

I love you!

Heather

Grandpa,

There are MANY things I love and admire about you, but I will just name a few.

The way you tease me. You always have something funny to say.

The way you are always working hard. You're always on the go.

How you take naps on the kitchen floor. Five beds and two couches and you sleep on the floor. ☺

I love you Grandpa and happy birthday.

Love,

Cynthia

My favorite memory of Grandpa is when we came up for his birthday and he was asleep. We sang to him and he jerked awake and we were afraid we might have given him a heart attack. Also, Grandpa shows a good example about good hard work. He still gets up and gets the chores done.

I love you!!!!!!!

Martha

I remember when you and Grandma were babysitting us and my friend came to walk with me to school and she was early, so Grandma said that I couldn't leave yet and you said, "They like to leave early so that they can take their time to walk to school." I just thought that that was funny.

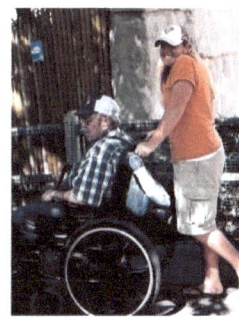 

Love,

Elizabeth

Kathryn

Memories of Dad – Verl Irvin Page

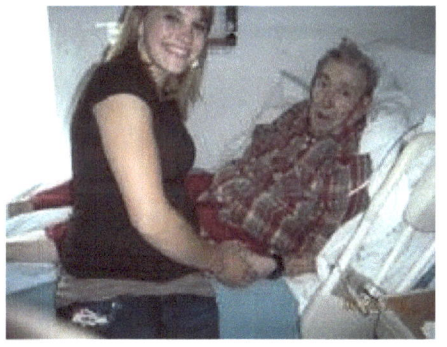

My earliest memories of Dad is when Uncle Keith died, first time I saw him cry. I remember picking up spuds on Uncle Keith's farm, but mostly I remember Dad putting me on the little A tractor and having me steer between the rows of gunny sacks of potatoes while Dad loaded the sacks on the flat trailer behind the tractor. At the end of the row he would run and jump on the tractor and turn to go back down the next rows of sacks.

I wasn't big enough or strong enough to turn the steering wheel fast enough to get turned around. This was probably the fall of 1958.

Most memories involve farm work – thinning, hoeing, topping, and loading beets; hauling hay, hauling syphon tubes, milking cows.

After we got the first station wagon it was a creamy tan color, Brett and I would get some blankets and pillows, lay down the seal and sleep in the car during the summer. Dad would need to go out to change the water during the middle of the night, so he would drive the station wagon out into the field. He never woke us up, but we would usually wake up. Especially when he'd leave the road to drive to which ever field he was irrigating.

Every summer the family would go to Hooper Springs in Soda Springs, Idaho. We'd have a picnic lunch and take jugs with us to fill with "Hooper water." Which was as close to soda as we got- except for the occasional bottle of A & W Root beer.

When my family moved to Rexburg, Dad & Mom would come up for a visit and we'd go to Yellowstone. Having Dad and Mom with us always made the Yellowstone visits more special and memorable. Through the 90's these were annual trips that my family enjoyed.

Janette

2002

Memories are funny things. Depending on the season or the current happening, different memories surface. Being that it is wintertime – and snowing today, along with the memories of having to do the chores in the snow, hauling in wood and coal and hauling out the ashes, feeding the calves, helping with the milking, I also remember the hood rides. You'd get an old car hood and tie it up behind one of the tractors. We'd bundle up and climb into the hood and hang on because you could really cut some tight corners.

Whether it was hauling hay (straw was easier) or thinning and hoeing the beets – we weren't sent out to work, you were right there with us. Along with all the work there are many other memories. I'm sure we appreciated the "free" time because there wasn't much of it. I really looked forward to those one day trips to the mountains for a picnic. Going to Hooper Springs in Soda Springs was a real treat.

I've lost track of the movies we went to, but we always went as a family. If we got there late, which happened often, we'd get to stay for the beginning because the theater always showed the movie twice. Sometimes we even got to see the second showing all the way through.

My family has really enjoyed having you and Mom come up and go with us to Yellowstone and Playmill. I'm' sure we get far more out of the trips because you and Mom are there with us.

I love you

Janette

Happy Birthday Grandpa

Things I remember about Grandpa,

When my family went to Salt Lake to drop Layne off at the MTC we stopped to have breakfast. At the restaurant there was a lady whose hair stood out on end. Grandpa leaned over to me and said, "It looks like she stuck her finger in a light socket." Then there was the time when he first saw my new glasses, for at that time they were new, Grandpa said that I got ripped off because I on only received half of a pair of glasses.

Always yours,

Nicholas

To Grandpa,

There are so many things that I have fond memories of spending time with you. I remember you telling me stories when we were out feeding the calves while Kelly milked. And when jumbuck got into the calves and made the calves jump the fence and you sticking jumpbuck with a pitchfork.

I thank you for letting me come and spend a week at the farm with you and Grandma. It was a good experience for me and very fun. I owe you a lot for all you taught me.

Love,

Orlan

My favorite memories of Grandpa by: Ila

He loves Maple-nuts

One thing is he always makes jokes.

Another thing is when he gave me dry shaves. Sometimes he still does it.

And the last thing (that I want to say) is when he caught like about 7 or so flies in his hand at one time.

I love you Grandpa

Love me,

Ila

Grandpa

I just wanted to tell you how much you mean to me. You have been such a positive influence in my life. You show your feelings and you're not afraid to. Like when you're upset with Grandma, you let he know. When you're sad, you cry. And when you're happy, you light up the whole room. You always make me laugh. And when I'm sad or in a bad situation, you can always make it better. Not just for me, but for all of your children, grandchildren and great grandchildren.

You're such a hard worker and you don't want help from others. I love that quality. That you can do it if you just try. I have learned so much from you. You have endured much pain and loss throughout your life, but it has made you a better and stronger person. I want to be like you, in being a hard worker and letting people know how I feel. (Unless it will hurt them☺) I love you so much and I hope that I can keep learning from you. Keep smiling, because you have a great smile. Again, I love you. Also, I hope that my children will be able to meet you and understand why I love you so much!

Love ya,

Ila

My Grandfather,

The peace maker of my family,

Yes, he's old,

Gray hair,

Wrinkled skin,

But he never give up.

Oh the joy he brings in my life.

The memories I have had with him,

I will never forget.

Sitting on his lap,

While he told me stories.

His hugs,

Oh so warming.

His advice,

"Never gets Old."

He always makes me laugh.

Haylee Lund

Dear Dad,

On your 80th birthday, I wanted to write you a letter and tell you how much I have appreciated working with you over the past 20 years.

My appreciation is two-fold; first I have really relied on your opinions concerning how to build something or when to cut hay or grain or bale hay or plant a crop of hay or corn. Like you used to say, "two heads are better than one." (Even if one is a cabbage head!) I never figured you were the cabbage head. Your direction in cropping decisions has been and still is greatly valued. Sometimes just being able to run ideas past you and talk about the problem, lended to finding the solutions. I miss those talks we had.

The second part of my appreciation is from the actual physical work you did to help me keep up with the farming. For example, I would bale hay just as long as I could and inevitably just before I had to sop to milk, move pipe or go to work then you would come and take over.

That extra hour or more sure makes a lot of difference in how fast we baled a field. That was one reason why I was able to last as long as I did because we were able to keep catch up with the farm work so I could take better care of the cattle. It didn't seem to bother you when I didn't always agree. You let me do things my way and was kind enough to not rub it in when my way didn't turn out like I had expected it to.

I had to have sons of my own to understand how hard that is for a dad to do. Thanks for your helping hands and ideas and thanks for letting me work with you for about 20 years.

I think that I am probably the luckiest son you have because of the time we spent together.

Thanks again so much,

Love, Brett

I really enjoyed the Sunday evening drives when we were growing and you telling us stories about people who lived in the houses which we passed.

One of the neat experiences that comes to mind right now is the one time we went deer hunting and you were driving Grandpa's old blue pickup. We went up through Dayton Canyon and clear around the back. Then you started driving up this pretty steep mountain. Fred Peterson was with us and he got pretty excited and wanted to get out and walk. I was really impressed with how well you could drive. You always could get tractors and cars unstuck better than anyone else I know.

Thanks for the years of working together; and especially for giving advice when I needed it. I'm sorry I couldn't figure out how to keep farming longer.

Thanks again,

Brett

Dad and Grandpa Page,

You were "Grandpa Page" before you were my "Dad" Page. So mostly our memories are of "Grandpa Page."

I remember how very delighted I was on the day that Brett and I were married that you got Brett all the way down to the Provo Temple. I can't tell you how relieved and extremely happy I was to see you there when we arrived.

When Greg had his first birthday, we all got to see him take his first steps... I'm sure the cheering you gave him, encouraged him to make a move.

I remember when Bryce died how supportive you and Grandma were as you waited at the hospital with us. It has meant so much to us that you so kindly gave us and Bryce his burial place. It was very special to us because we knew that you knew much more about how we were feeling than we did. What a wonderful time it was or a special time it was when you laid your hands upon Brett's head and gave him a father's blessing after Bryce's funeral.

One of my very favorite memories was when you and grandma returned from you church history tour for your 50th anniversary. I saw a sparkle and a twinkle in your eye that was brighter than I had noticed before. We knew that you have a special love for Grandma and it showed all over. You seemed like you had just fallen in love for the first time...all over again. It was neat to see your countenance shine as we saw your love for Grandma come through that way.

You have given us some nice memories.

Thank you for sharing with us.

Love,

Rosaline

I am thankful for the opportunity to grow up near Grandpa's Farm. I remember feeding the calves with Grandpa. We would mix up the powdered milk replacement to feed the calves – it smelled funny. Then we'd go to the calf shed, located to the side of the new house and dump the milk replacement in a trough for the calves. There was a little water spout that supplied the calves with water. Grandpa always told Greg and I not to drink out of it. But we didn't listen; it was fun to feel the sting of water up our noses. A little canal water never hurt.

I loved spending Thanksgiving at Grandma and Grandpa's with all my aunts, uncles and cousins. I especially loved the hood rides Grandpa took us on. Afterwards he hitched an old automobile hood cover onto the red Massey Ferguson. We hopped on and held on for dear life as we sped across the drive way or the field across from the house. What a blast!!! The cold wind bit my nose and ears, and my poor bottom was sore afterwards. It was worth the adrenaline rush that only Grandpa's hood rides provide.

One sensation that stays with me is the feel of Grandpa's whiskers when he would give me "whisker kisses." His stubble was prickly and tickly against my soft cheek; and sometimes his cheeks were cold from doing the outside chores. A true treasure.

Grandpa is one of the best story tellers I know. His eyes lit up and the excitement in his voice—I love to hear him depict stories of the Merchant Marines. But my favorite stories had to do with the outhouses. (I don't remember exactly how the story went but some boys were sure disappointed that they didn't pull off a prank.)

What I love most about my Grandpa Page is that he's an all-around incredible person. Grandpa taught me the value of hard work by his example. He did his darnedest to provide his family with a decent living. He sacrificed so that his children would have a better life. He lives the gospel. I never heard Grandpa bear his testimony of the Gospel, but his actions told all. I'm blessed to have such a beautiful person for a teacher, an example, a friend, a Grandpa.

I love you Grandpa Page. I with you the best birthday and joyful memories.

Love,

Lisa

Grandpa,

Thank you for all that you have done for me as well as our family. I can't tell you how much I appreciate you being there.

Ben

One thing I remember about Grandpa is his stories. My favorite one is when he tells about how Grandma fainted at a dance when they first met. He told me this story after I fainted at Aunt Janette's house a few summers ago.

I also remember how he always smiles whenever he sees me or another one of his grandkids. I like that because it shows he has love and consideration for each one of us.

One of my favorite things he used to say to me was, "Watch out for those sneaky crops. The corn has ears and the potatoes have eyes."

Danette ☺

Dad,

I remember you taking us and going fishing by Twin Lakes at the Chubb Hole. I loved and still love sitting on your lap. You would take us on car rides to different places and that was very fun. You took us to American Falls, Idaho to see Grandma Murri and my cousins. Dad took us to the Big Page Family Reunions.

You taught me how to work hard. I remember that one time I was cleaning the milk tank and I screamed because I was happy and you came running, probably because you thought something was wrong. You let Kelly and I go with the milk man on his route which was a daylong event. I learned how to hoe beets and pick up potatoes. Dad found a rattlesnake and cut off his head and the snake rattles still rattled. When Clyde was set apart for his mission we went to A & W afterwards.

Dad let me play in the band and go on all the band trips.

One time we went to Salt Lake to take one of my brothers or sisters to serve on a mission and we were stopped on the freeway because of construction. A man had some kittens and didn't know what to do with them and Dad let us bring them home.

For a Family Home Evening that Dad was in charge of, Dad said that we could choose anything from the storage to have for supper. Dad choose bottled dewberries.

Dad and Mom went with Gordon and I to California for one of Gordon's friends weddings. We were able to go to Disneyland and have fun. Dad let my 3 boys stay with him while Gordon and I went to Alaska in 2000.

Gordon and I with the kids would drive Dad and Mom at Christmas time to see the Christmas Lights in Preston and Logan. Gordon and I took them to Rexburg and we went to see where Mom was born and the cemetery where Grandpa and Grandma Murri are buried.

I know that I am the favorite because I am named after Dad and Mom. Or you just couldn't think up anymore names.

Love,

Verna

Dear Grampa,

I had fun last year with the cows. And it was fun, but hard.

The end.

Reed age 14

I remember when Grandpa sat in his big chair and we watched a movie.

Love,

Camille age 11

Dear Grandpa,

I like the cows and the tractors. They are fun. I like them they are nice,

Byron age 9

Grandpa is working on the farm, fun or not.

 Skyler

Some of Kelly's memories,

Going fishing at the chub hole on Monday night for family home evening. Weiner roast in the summer in the back yard. Going for a drive up Stockton the afternoon after the last load of hay is hauled and stacked in the yard. Going to American Falls on Thanksgiving Day to visit the cousins. And of course family reunions in July.

Getting the cows milked early on opening day of deer hunting. Being up on Rattlesnake Mountain at sun up. Brett and I milking the cows early on Christmas morning so dad could have the morning off if he wanted.

Kelly

I remember when I needed some help with my bike and Grandpa helped me with my problem and that helped me a lot and that's one of the memories I remember

Also I remember when I was having a problem with something and Grandpa made it easier for me to do and it helped me a lot and that's another memory I remember.

Love Kody

When I came to see Grampa, I like to say hi and I like to give him hugs.

Love KC

Grandma and Grandchildren - Grandpa's Hats Jan. 19, 2015

Here you can add your own memories.

Travel

Here are some of the places that Verl and Helena traveled during their married life. Of course Verl traveled in the Merchant marines too.

1946, Our Honeymoon Yellowstone Park.

Our first trip was 1960. We went to Rosemead, CA, where my sister Esther and Dale Ehrisman lived. For the marriage of my sister Ina Mae to James Sanders, September 1960.

1964 or 1965 Yellowstone, Clyde stayed home and took care of the farm. This was the summer before Shalene would leave for college and we wanted to have a family vacation.

1971 We went to Mtn. Home, Idaho and visited Maurice and Idella Murri.

January of 1976 Helena went to Mundelein, IL, to help Shalene and Ron as Shalene had to have her tonsils out and had 18 month old Paul.

1976 Verl and Helena went to San Gabriel, California with Lyn and Hilda Murri (where sister Esther and Dale Ehrisman lived, and from there Spring Valley, Near San Diego for Helena's brother, Cyril Jean's Memorial Service.

1976 November after Brett returned home from his mission, he took care of the farm while we took a trip to Arizona to see Vera and then we drove on to Texas to visit with Clyde and Dixie.

California trip with Ina Mae saw Paul on his mission and many other sights in San Francisco.

1985 We rode with Lyn and Hilda Murri to Franklin, OH, for the funeral of Standley Jeffrey. Helena's sister, Leda's husband.

1986 We rode with Verna and Gordon to Los Angeles, CA. Gordon served his mission in Orange County and was able to arrange for us to stay with a Chinese family that he knew. We went to Disneyland and to a session in the Los Angeles Temple, while Verna and Gordon attended a sealing of a friend.

Circa 1993 or 1994 Ogden Canyon Dinosaur Park, Kamas and Francis to cemeteries to see Page Ancestors, Dinosaur Land in Vernal, Flaming Gorge, Fort Bridger, Star Valley – Call Museum to an Airplane Show., Evanston to a railroad show and then to Rexburg to see Janette and then home.

1995 Craters of the moon with Janette and family.

1996 Our children gave us a Church History Tour for our 50th Anniversary.

June 28, 1997 West Yellowstone with Janette and girls.

May 30, 1998 West Yellowstone with Janette and girls.

April 1999, Theron Atkinson died and Shalene drove us to Casagrande, Arizona for the funeral.

June 3, 1999 West Yellowstone with Janette and girls.

1999 We chaperoned Clyde and Terri when they went to the Spokane while the temple was being built. Terri's brother was the foreman for the building. We drove through Montana and down through Boise

June 1, 2000 West Yellowstone with Janette and girls.

2000 We accompanied Clyde and his family to Rapid City, South Dakota for Barbershop. We drove to Rexburg to get Heather, then on to Cody, Wyoming and Dead Wood City, South Dakota. In Casper, Wyoming we attended the Conference Center Dedication. We had our lunch in the kitchen of the church.

June 1, 2001 West Yellowstone with Janette and girls.

2001 we went to Nashville for barbershop in Jul. We drove via Winters Quarters, NE, Nauvoo, IL, Carthage, IL, St. Louis, MO and on to Nashville, TN. On the way home we went the other direction through battle grounds in GA, Oklahoma, Texas, etc.

2001 September, we flew to Nashville for the marriage of our oldest grandson, Nathan.

2002 We went to the Olympics in Salt Lake City, UT.

2002 West Yellowstone with Janette and girls.

May 31, 2003 West Yellowstone with Janette and girls.

2003 Portland Barbershop trip. Clyde drove his 15 passenger van to Portland Oregon and then down the west coast. Here we got to see the Redwood Forest, Winston Oregon Safari, rode an elephant, beaches along the West Coast, etc.

2003 trip to Yellowstone Park, doing the whole two loops.

Ila and Hailey Lund would perform in Playmill theatre in West Yellowstone every June while they were young. We also went with them to Craters of the Moon.

2004 Barbershop in the Conference Center

Dairy Duz it!

The End of an ERA for Verl and Helena Page -2006

Cows and dairying have been in Verl's entire life to this date—May 25, 2006. This story has its beginning in 1919 at the marriage of James Irvin and Lareta McCombs Page. They were married on 19 Nov. 1919 and were given a part-breed Jersey cow for a wedding present, named Star, from Lareta's parents, Peter Exekiel and Mary Ann Goody McCombs. When Star, the cow, was about to go dry, Irvin would have Verl milk her at the night milking. Verl says he was about 3 years old when he began learning how to hand milk a cow. (or Cows) both morning and night milkings with his father. Until the Page family moved onto the farm before 1928, George Balls, a neighbor, gave Verl and Don a bull calf which they raised, then traded for a 1 day-old heifer calf to raise for their own cow and a number was put on their milk can for their own income.

On the farm, a barn was built for 14 cows, using 13 stalls and 1 space left for the milk cans to be filled. The milk was carried to another building where there was a separator used to separate the cream from the milk. The milk was fed to the pigs and the cream sold in Preston to either Weber Creamery on 1st West or at another creamery by the Axel Johnson Blacksmith Shop on State Street (south of present-day Valley Implement.) Cows were milked by hand until about 1940 or 1941 when Air lines were installed for Surge Milker pails.

Verl and Helena were given a small black cow for a wedding present from his father, Irvin, which was the beginning of a dairy herd that lasted 60 years. After about 1950, we got 10 heifers from Irvin which increased the herd to 17 head. We had built a barn of railroad ties obtained from railroad tracks in Fairview. About 1953, Clyde, a 3-year old, remembers the men nailing the roof on the barn. Now the barn could hold our growing herd, more than could be milked in the chicken coop which had held 6 cows. Instead of hand milking, Verl milked with a little red vacuum pump on the wall run with belts for 2 units of Surge milkers. Verl tied cows to the wall of the holding shed to hand milk them until the stanchions were built in the new barn. At about this time, 1955, we purchased 2 Surge pails/milkers with a vacuum pump,

dumped the milk into milk cans in the doorway, the wheeled the cans to a cement trough we built. The trough was filled with water daily to keep the milk cold. Even then, we seemed to have milk come back from the Morning Milk Company in Wellsville, This made some of the very best cottage cheese a family could eat (made mostly from cream), because the milk was picked up early and not cooled, then hauled all the way around the milk route. For a time, we sold our milk to Pet Milk Company in Preston. Sometime after we moved to live across the road in Dec. 1965, we began to sell milk to Ed Gossner's, as he came to our home to solicit milk for his company. He said he wouldn't under-
pay us and wanted to buy our milk which was better for us to get paid. By 1967, we were milking 32 cows.

It soon become apparent to keep up with progress and demand, that we had to build a milk house, install a pipeline and tank to handle the milk so it would be kept cold until hauled by a tank truck to the milk plant. On 25 May 1972, the men poured the cement floor for the milk house. On 26 Jun, they took the wooden wall out of the barn, put forms in where they poured 4 yards of cement. Shale was hauled from Dayton Canyon for the corral and holding shed, then cement poured in the shed on 5 Jul. On 26 Jul, cement was poured in the corral and barn gutter. From 14 Aug to 18 Aug, Glen Carlson laid concrete blocks for the milk house. We purchased lumber, sheeting, and roofing materials. Through Sep and Oct, the men put on the metal roof, worked on the doors and windows, the ridge roll on the roof, installed the gable ends and worked on the ceiling, all this being done in 1972.

From 13 Mar 1973 to 3 Apr, Alan Law and Ellis Gilbert came and put the milk tank in, installed the pump, and worked continuously on the milker equipment so all would work and have no problems. On 4 Apr, milking was done with the pipeline for the milk to go into the tank for the first time. We sent our 1st tank of milk to Gossner's on 7 Apr 1973. After most of the harvest of crops was done, more shale was hauled for the corral, then cement was poured before winter. Verl's father, Irvin, spent a lot of hours
building the cow shed for their protection from the heat and cold. By late Nov that year, the cow shed was complete with stalls and gates.

We have had several mishaps handling cows. One in particular happened on 5 Nov 1973. We had the cows in the field behind the pea viner to feed off the remaining hay or grain before winter. As we were gathering the cows together, one got Verl down and tramped on him, mostly on his legs. He lost his glasses and Janette remembers that she helped find them. Three days later, he went to the Dr. for pills to thin his blood so he wouldn't get a blood clot. Helena remembers that he had to go to the hospital daily for several times to have his blood checked and Verl recovered from that experience.

With the help of Brett and Kelly, the herd increased to about 80 head of cows. About 1987, we split the herd with Brett for his grade-A dairy at his farm across the street from

his Grandpa Irvin Page farm. In Jun 1994, we were featured in the Dairy Edition of the Preston Citizen Paper. The article and photos of this feature are included at the end of this story. Not much changed with the dairy which was maintained at about 40 cows, as we were able to raise most of the hay, grain and corn silage for that size herd. Verl had to quit doing the milking, but fed the calves morning and night until about 2004 when he had hip replacement surgery on 19 Apr 2004. Since then, Kelly has shouldered the dairy responsibilities. Because of lower milk prices, rising feed and operating costs, less replacements and death of some cows, we decided it was time to close this era of our lives. On 25 and 26 May, 2006, all cows and steers were sold. No more cows getting out in the middle of the night and at many other times. too. Having to stand still so a bull wouldn't attack and having to ring and chain them for safety in the corral.

Unfortunately, there is no more cream for home-made ice-cream and whole milk for the breakfast cereal. Who of the children remembers playing with the milk cart that we used to move the filled milk cans from the barn to the cooler? Who remembers having to get up early to help milk as an older sibling was serving his/her mission? Who got up early, helped milk then went to practice basketball before school? Who didn't like to help milk cows but did it anyway, because you were taught to work together as a family? Why did Clyde stay home to do chores, farm work so that the rest of the family could go to Yellowstone Park on their one and only family vacation in 1965? Because we worked together as a family for the betterment of each other. When Verl and Helena went to funerals or weddings, it was the children who took care of the milking and other chores for us to do so. Janette remembers spending the summer before her mission milking cows

as well as taking care of the house while Helena was in summer school at USU. Helena remembers helping with standing in the door to move the cows into their stalls when a cow hit the door, injuring her hand and fainting on the floor of the breezeway. She also took her turn at shoveling grain to the cows, cleaning the gutter, washing milkers, and more sometimes so that the work would be done. I am sure there are many more memories of life on the farm associated with the dairy. Without the dairy it would have been impossible to send 6 on missions and all to receive some college education. This has come together on the eve of our 60th wedding anniversary and what a significant coincidence for all of this to happen this year. We leave this story as a legacy to each of you, our children, for you to share with your children and grandchildren as you wish. The source of this story is personal knowledge of Verl and Helena and Verl's Diaries in his possession.

Written by Helena Page, 12 June 2006

Honors for lifetime resident of Dayton – July 4, 2009 – Verl Page

(At the 4th of July Celebration in Dayton, Citizens have been honored for their dedicated service to the community.)

The person honored today was born in Riverdale, Idaho at the home of his Grandmother. From the day he was brought home to his Parent's Dayton home, he spent the remainder of his life here, except for a year serving in the Merchant Marines. When he was a child, he went to gather eggs in the barn. As he was climbing into the manger, a gray horse his father owned, reached out and bit him on the side of his face. He was rushed to the Doctor in Preston and it took 13 stitches to sew that side of his cheek in place. After surgery, he lived with his grandmother in Preston, they would walk to the Dr. Office to have the wound cleaned and dressed.

When he was about 10 or 11 years old, he wore his father's shoes to the canyon to get their winters wood because his shoes were worn out. His father wore his irrigating boots. He attended school in Dayton and graduated from Weston High School in 1941. He worked on the family farm after graduating, being deferred from the military, but in the summer of 1945 he received his draft notice. So he and 2 other young men of Dayton took a bus to Salt Lake City and enlisted in the Merchant Marines. On 19 July 1945, with basic training at Catalina Island, he sailed as a water tender on an oil tanker along the West Coast, to Alaska, Aleutian Islands and Hawaii.

He returned home to Dayton in March 1946, got married and spent the next 30 years farming with his father. Using the same farm equipment as that was the economical way to operate farms. He acquired more land in order to provide a living for the family of 7 children, as well as feed for the increased dairy herd. Later with his sons, they continued farming together and operating a dairy until 2006, being in the dairy business for 60 years. Farming practices were in transition in the late 1940's from horses to mechanized farming. He loved driving a tractor. He said, "I think the best talent I had was learning to drive a tractor...my dad always scolded me because I couldn't drive the horses and make them do what he wanted them to do."

He served in different capacities in the Dayton Ward until the wards were re-aligned in 1981, serving as Secretary in the Aaronic Priesthood, Home Teacher Supervisor and Home Teacher, Sunday School Secretary and served as Superintendent for 4 years from 1969 to 1973. He was of service in the ward helping other Priesthood leaders obtain flour from Richmond and delivering 8050 lbs. to ward members. He helped put up Christmas lights on the church house.

He was elected on the Dayton, Linrose Cemetery Board November 1969 and served faithfully for 30 years until November 1999, serving as Chairman for several years beginning in April 1974. He served with two other dedicated men, Carl Bingham and Perry Phillips. He was on call to help mark graves, plow out the snow in winter and assist with the burials in the cemetery, when needed. He deserves to be honored as a lifelong member of the Dayton Community and the family appreciates him being recognized by the Dayton City Council for this honor.

We would like to thank all of those who have helped with this project. Their contributions are appreciated.

This closes the life of a wonderful, honest, upright man of integrity, who truly is of the Greatest Generation.

www.ingramcontent.com/pod-product-compliance
Lightning Source LLC
Chambersburg PA
CBHW040100160426
43193CB00002B/28